AF575139

One Kingdom

ONE KINGDOM

OUR LIVES WITH ANIMALS

THE HUMAN-ANIMAL BOND IN MYTH,

HISTORY, SCIENCE,

AND STORY

by

DEBORAH NOYES

HOUGHTON MIFFLIN COMPANY
BOSTON 2006

Nineteenth-century line art by Georges Cuvier
Excerpt from "The Long Loneliness" from *The Star Thrower*
by Loren Eiseley, Harcourt, 1979

www.houghtonmifflinbooks.com

Book design by Michael Nelson
The text of this book is set in Kennerley.
The photographs are gelatin silver prints.

Library of Congress Cataloging-in-Publication Data
Noyes, Deborah.
One kingdom : our lives with animals / by Deborah Noyes.
p. cm.
ISBN 0-618-49914-8 (hardcover)
1. Human-animal relationships. 2. Animals—Psychological aspects. I. Title.
QL85.N69 2006
590—dc22
2005025446

ISBN-13: 978-0618-49914-4

Manufactured in China
SCP 10 9 8 7 6 5 4 3 2 1

For Michaela—my wild one—
with love

CONTENTS

ONE KINGDOM

INTRODUCTION

Summer has me thinking about water. Not just its shimmering skin or the foam edge at my feet, littered with sea glass and egg casings, but what the water holds: the glint of scales in streaky light, the scuttle of claw and groping tentacle, and, deeper still, the inky, unexplored depths. I'm thinking too of our skins and what they hold—water, blood and bone, a beating heart—and things shapeless and vast: identity, spirit, memory.

In the folklore of the northern coasts of Scotland, Ireland, and Iceland, creatures called selkies haunt the shallows, basking along rocky shoreline in the form of seals. On land they lumber, but selkies are swift and sleek in the waves, and if, on Midsummer Eve, you brave a craggy shoreline, you might see the bob and gleam of their dark heads among the rocks or even witness a breathtaking transformation. Up they flop on shore, barking and coughing, and in a wink they've left their sealskins puddled on stone, emerging as beautiful young women. All night these maidens dance and sing, eerily, until the stars blink out. Then they wriggle back into mottled velvet skins, tip into the sea, and vanish as if they'd never been.

In some versions of this story, a mortal man gets a good look but does more than stand there rapt. He snatches up one dancer's pelt before she can retreat. Holding it tight, he leads her home to be his bride, ignoring her tears and pleadings. He hides the sealskin with care and cunning.

And so the selkie is stranded with little choice but to become a faithful wife and later, a loving (if remote—with that habit of staring off at the sea) mother. Her young husband means well and loves her well. He dresses her in the finest garments his farmer's wage will allow, weaving flowers he's coaxed from the earth into her hair. Each night, after she lulls their children to sleep, he begs his wife to sing her strange, sweet songs for him, and she does so gladly, though he may wake later to find her out pacing the cliffs, her long hair blown forward to mask the human tears.

One morning when her husband has gone to harvest with the light still coppery pink in the east, their youngest child races down from the hills with a limp shape draped over her arms. "What have you found, little one?" asks the mother, her eyes wide and dark. "You have been digging. Give it here. How fine and soft it looks."

The child comes forth, and the young mother kisses the soiled fingers one by one, hungrily, and holds both child and sealskin close. The little girl wriggles free and skips away. When her father later asks where Mother has gone, she says not a word but points toward the sea, and he knows at once their loss.

The seals in such lore are not seals, of course, or human, but some elusive fairy hybrid. Being able to traipse in and out of your skin at will is a feat, to be sure, but the selkie has always fascinated me less for what she can do than for what she is: strange. Utterly so. She lives without walls in a home miles and watery miles wide; her blood beats to a different, tidal pulse; her lips are salty, and her teeth, even under sweet pink lips, can slice through scales.

I recognize this otherness now, but I used to wonder: How could she abandon her children? Didn't she wish to be cared for, sheltered, loved? Wouldn't it bring her grief to leave?

But now I understand. She is a selkie. She might endure her human costume, relent a little—like a dog tossed a biscuit or a dolphin a sardine—but try as she will to change for our sakes, she can *be* only what she is. Believing otherwise will lead to heartbreak. So I've given the selkie back her skin.

And because it seems like the best way to know them, I'm trying to do the same for dog and dolphin, ape and elephant, heron and hog—to see them for what they are and not what I want them to be. But it's hard work, because one habit of our human nature is to seek and find in other species, always and instead, ourselves.

• • •

From our earliest beginnings, animals showed up in our myths and folklore as gods and omens, appeared in cave paintings and constellations, and were the gifts of kings and the tools of generals and empire builders. We not only endowed them with human traits in our tales, but in some cases, like the selkie, we literally married our own aspect with theirs.

From Minotaur, centaur, and satyr to mermaid and werewolf, world mythology and folklore swarm with strange and fabulous human-animal hybrids, right up through modern comic-book superpowers like Batman, Catwoman, and Spider-Man. Did we dream them up to glorify what was best in animals and the wild, or to point out the worst in ourselves? To show how bound we are to other species? Or to caution *against* our animal natures . . .

One thing seems clear. We want to know them. Whether the goal is to conserve or consume them, talk to or train them, befriend or master them—animals matter to us. They have always mattered to us. It's our ongoing task and our privilege to ask, "Who are you?"

As small children, we identify and long to communicate with other species, and our longings find fast fuel in picture books, TV shows, and movies peopled with talking beasts. From the day we get our first teddy bear or set out on pleasing adventures with Paddington and Pooh, we learn to see animals as people with fur (or feathers or scales). Scientists call the tendency to find the human in the seal (or dog or bear) anthropomorphizing. We anthropomorphize by lending human traits or characteristics to nonhuman animals or objects.

As toddlers we howl like wolves, lumber like elephants, hop like rabbits, and in general delight in mimicking the gestures and noises of the barnyard and jungle, but as we grow, our need to communicate draws us deeper into the mysteries of other people—our parents, siblings, peers. And, animals aside, it's hard enough to get a read on what another human being is thinking or feeling, even with our shared gift for language.

Because we can't communicate with animals directly, we're left to wonder, are they sentient (that is, conscious)? Do they think and feel as we do? To what degree? And *what* do they think? What do they feel?

Knowing them, it turns out, is harder than it seems.

Part 1

A Brief History

Beasts and Shadows: Early Days

Humans have always shared a bond with animals, but imagine how intense that bond must have been for earlier humans, who survived by gathering wild plants and hunting the huge herds of horses, bison, reindeer, and mammoth that roamed tundra and grasslands. These people knew and planned for animal migration routes. They attacked outright with axes and spears or lured animals into snares and pits, ambushing entire herds by stampeding them over cliffs. Their dreams must have been bloody, shimmering with teeth and claws and pounding hooves. Near life-size Paleolithic paintings of Stone Age prey have been discovered all over Europe at sites like Lascaux in France and Altamira in Spain.

These hunter-gatherers lived in nomadic family groups or clans, ranging from place to place and building temporary camps in concert with the seasons and the flow of game. They would have used every part of a kill, cooking the meat or preserving it, shaping hides into cloth, burning animal fat in lamps, crafting bones and antlers into tools and weapons. These implements they decorated with carvings of their prey, even as they wore the skins and charms of predators they admired. Early humans depended on animals, and they knew it. You might say they repaid the debt by holding animals sacred.

The term *animism* comes from the Latin word *anima,* meaning "breath" or "soul," and is the idea that a soul or spirit resides in every object. Anthropologists say that animism, one of the oldest forms of human belief dating back to the Paleolithic age, originated so primitive people could make sense of certain mysteries: Why do we see pictures when we sleep? How do we distinguish sleep from death? What animates a body, and where does that life force go when the body dies?

For early humans, who lived in close contact with nature, a world of spirits made perfect sense. If everything has a soul, then all things are charged and sacred, worthy of respect. In a world where trees and plants—valued for their usefulness and beauty—might also house powerful nymphs or dryads, a pagan woodcutter would do well to beg forgiveness before wielding the ax.

In an animistic world, even inanimate objects such as stones might lodge souls, so it's no surprise that animals—so vital, dazzling in their diversity—captured our imagination from the start. World mythology is full of animal spirits, gods, and demons. Honored for their strength, speed, and fertility, animals made handy symbols. We situated them in our creation myths and in the sky, naming constellations after them. We made them tribal totems and formed cults around them—especially the dangerous ones, as the soul of a slain beast might return to exact vengeance on the hunter. Humans must have hoped to placate powerful predators, too, by granting them sacred status.

Tricky Symbols

Sometimes animals help establish a social order, and sometimes, as symbols, they subvert or threaten it. Many cultures have tales of animal tricksters who break the rules of the gods or of nature, often through tricks and thievery. Tricksters can be sly or foolish or both, but they're almost always amusing, even when they're up to serious mischief. They do and say the things we'd like to do and say, fight the powers that be and (usually) win, and even when they're less than kind, we love them for their wit and daring. The Monkey King, Sun Wukong, a beloved figure in classical Chinese literature, wreaked havoc in Heaven. In North American lore, Raven stole light; Coyote stole fire. Anansi the spider is a famous trickster-god of West African lore.

Spirit-Lore and Superstition

Animals have always helped humans explain the inexplicable—not least our fears. In many (though not all) cultures, for instance, owls were deemed bad omens, their hoots mournful, their image tied to death or ill fortune. The Aztecs associated the bird with Techlotl, god of the dead, and the Chinese believed that owls snatched the soul away. The Pimas, a tribe of the southwestern United States, also aligned owls with death and the soul, and gave owl feathers to a dying person to help him into the next world. If a Pima family had none, they procured feathers—those of a freshly caught owl were best—from the tribe's medicine man.

It's no coincidence that owls are nocturnal. Even today, we're wary of creatures of the night, it seems. For one thing, they're awake when we're not, when we can't keep an eye on them. Even in metal cars and sturdy dwellings built of brick, armed with our locks and our reason, we still flinch at the gaze glowing in the headlights or the flitting of a bat. When we venture out of bed for a glass of water, our feet cold and vulnerable on the kitchen tiles, the darting shadow of a house mouse can still evoke an almost primal response. Imagine how our ancestors felt—exposed to predators and the elements, hemmed in only by a ring of firelight. It's no wonder our race wove an explanatory web of spirit-lore and superstition around a world of beasts and shadows. Omens and other "irrational" notions about animals have always addressed our deepest fears. Perhaps, too, they help ease them.

Some Pacific Islanders worshiped sharks, erecting stone altars in their honor and holding shark-kissing ceremonies to earn spiritual protection for their swimming areas. In some cultures, meanwhile—like those of the Naskapi caribou hunters in the Canadian arctic or the reindeer hunters in Siberia—a prey animal might be seen as a willing participant in its own death. The hunter gains the animal's meat, hide, and bones, but its spirit lives on in a cycle of death and rebirth, and the hunter must beware not to offend that spirit since disrespect or ridicule threaten the future supply of game. The idea of atoning for a life taken was common in many hunting cultures and persists even today.

The Last Monsters

Even today we view the big predators—bleak, magnificent, often solitary hunters like shark, tiger, leopard, and crocodile—with a kind of terrible awe. They impress and humble us, and have had our wrath to show for it. In recent times we've pushed many to or over the edge of extinction, perhaps because they recall for us what it must have been like (and still is in some few remote places) for our long-ago ancestors. To be hunter and hunted. To be stalked and savaged, reduced to meat. Our race may take refuge in reason, and in scientific and technological dominance, but these bold predators are in many ways the last "monsters" on earth, challenging our assumption that we reign alone at the top of the food chain.

To be a successful hunter (or avoid becoming prey) you have to know the habits of your quarry (or how to outmaneuver a predator). Where will it make its den, and when does it breed? What are its territorial and seasonal movements? What does it eat, and where does it find drinking water? You need to inhabit the animal for a time and see the world from its point of view, inviting empathy.

About 10,000 years ago, the global climate began to change, gradually warming. Forest replaced grasslands, and due to this and other factors, such as overhunting, the great herds of grazing animals vanished. As forest spread over the land, men began to hunt with bow and arrow, and by about 12,000 B.C., people were using tame dogs in the chase, though it would be another 2,000 years or so before they fully domesticated them.

By 8000 B.C. or so, people in the Near East were beginning to grow their own food, a feat that would dramatically change the course of human history. Instead of just gathering the seeds of wild grasses, they put some aside, planting them the next year to yield a crop. Humans, nomadic hunters for so long, began to work the land. They settled in one place to tend crops and guard the harvest.

What's more, people began to domesticate wild animals. Wild sheep, goats, pigs, and cattle had been hunted for thousands of years before humans took to rounding them into pens, which made them easier to catch. The first animals to be kept

Old Men in Fur Coats

The more like us an animal seems—or the more symbolically linked to our struggles and survival—the more we seem to respect it. Bears are easy to anthropomorphize. They often walk upright, for one thing, and a hunter I know confirmed that in size and shape, a skinned bear looks eerily human.

Many primitive cultures dreaded impending winter, when the flora and fauna around them began to die off or disappear. Winter is a vivid symbol of death, and bears—which appear to vanish into the earth in winter, magically resurfacing with spring—embodied the cycle of life and death for many cultures of the Northern Hemisphere. In fact, bear cults are still thought to exist in remote parts of the world. The bear hunter in such cultures might view his prey as spiritual kin, with grave respect, and take pains to avoid offending the bear or calling it by name, relying instead on nicknames like Grandfather, Angry One, or Old Man in a Fur Coat. Killing a bear was a sacred act, and ideally the hunter used a spear, club, or other traditional weapon, cornering the bear in a stand-up fight before apologizing and reporting the reason for the kill. He might even skirt responsibility by finger pointing: "It wasn't I, Grandfather, it was [insert enemy's name here] who made use of me to kill you. I am sorry!"

In some cultures, such as the Ainu people of mountainous Japan, if hunters found a mother bear with a cub, they killed the adult female and carried the cub home to their village. There it was raised by a childless couple, which nursed it and treated it as an honored guest, perhaps even allowing the cub to claim a bed. It might be released into the forest after three years or kept and raised to adulthood and then ritually sacrificed. For the Ainu, who held their bear celebration in early December, the bear wasn't an earthly creature at all but a temporary visitor from the spirit world who longed to return there. The Ainu hunted the bear to trigger this metamorphosis, and *to sacrifice* in their language means "to send away."

this way were probably sheep and goats around 8500 B.C. in the Near East. Chickens were eventually domesticated for their meat and eggs. The llama was kept for meat and wool in South America, along with the alpaca, ducks, and guinea pigs. In Southeast Asia, pigs were an important resource. Regular contact with people made these creatures tamer.

In due course, herders noticed that larger animals often had larger young, so they let only these animals breed, and over time, domestic animals became bigger and stronger than wild ones. Humans saw that all dogs, for instance, are not the same. Some sport strength and endurance, some run fast, others are fighters. In time, people bred dogs to have select traits, crafting hunting, herding, and guard dogs for themselves. This careful breeding is called animal husbandry.

By about 2000 B.C., all of our most important domestic plants and animals were an established fact of human society. As farming caught on, the traditional culture of hunting and gathering faded. There's no doubt these changes altered daily life forever. But did the shift from hunting to agriculture and husbandry change the way humans *thought* about animals?

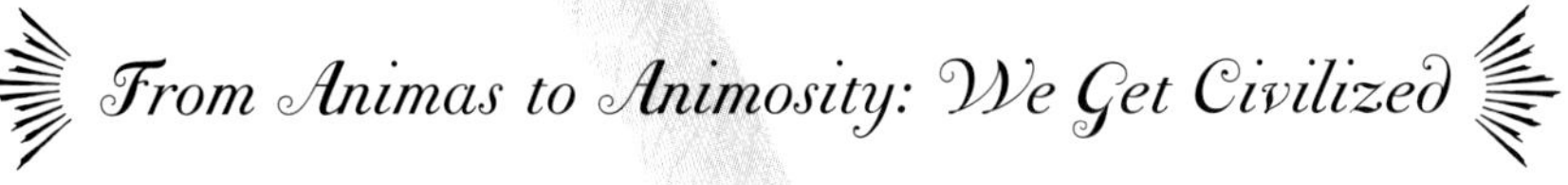

From Animas to Animosity: We Get Civilized

When Howard Carter first thrust a candle into the unearthed tomb of Tutankhamen—the Egyptian pharaoh better known as King Tut—the archaeologist got an eyeful of gold and "wonderful things." Among this inventory were a stone lion, a stool with legs carved to mimic the slender necks of geese, and furniture engraved with "monstrous animals." Decorated figures, pendants, and alabaster jars revealed a bird emerging from an egg, a kneeling ibis, winged scarab beetles, a vulture-goddess, and the jackal-headed god Anubis. All would do their part to ease Tut's passage to the afterlife. There was also, of course, the boy king himself with a tangle of gold cobras cupping his brow and shaved head.

The ancient Egyptians believed in a world system established by Ra, the sun god, who took different forms from a scarab beetle to a hawk. All creatures played a part in the eternal cosmic drama, and the Egyptians worshiped hundreds of animal-headed gods and goddesses. Usually these beasts of religious and symbolic significance—like hippo and crocodile—were central to daily life in the Nile Valley. Cats were sacred to the Egyptian goddess Bastet, who was usually depicted with the head of a cat. According to the ancient historian Herodotus, Egyptians who hurt or hassled a cat could be punished by death. When a cat died, family members shaved off their eyebrows in mourning and held grand funeral processions, entombing the mummified feline with favored toys and plates of food or a feast of tiny (also mummified) mice to nourish it in the afterlife.

Ancient Egyptians worshiped and respected the animal kingdom in many ways, but their "animal" deities had human bodies. Why? Did animals make less-than-satisfactory gods because people had no direct line of communication with them? Perhaps pairing a distinct animal "nature" (most easily identified by the head) with a human torso (for the Egyptians, the heart was the organ of intellect) was as much a way of ensuring discourse between the human and animal as it was a marriage of the earthly and the divine worlds.

• • •

In the late nineteenth century,

archaeologists uncovered more than 300,000 cat mummies

at a single dig site in Beni Hassan, Egypt.

Other advanced civilizations, such as the ancient Greeks and Romans, were at least as likely to hold animals suspect as to make them gods. In the first century B.C., the Roman poet Lucretius complained that Earth was "greedily possessed by mountains and the forest of wild beasts." Like many people then, he believed humans had defeated fear and uncertainty through agriculture, city walls, weaponry, shipping, roads, and other feats of civilization.

In the lore of the time, the wild world was terrifying, a shelter for hideous supernatural beings and man-eating ogres. Even the forest god Pan exuded menace, triggering "panic" in people who braved remote landscapes. The god Dionysus was formidable because he'd been reared among—and could tame—even the fiercest beasts. For the ancient Greeks and Romans, the wild and all that lived there were at best competition for resources. At worst, they were a threat to be dominated.

One way of displaying control over wild nature was to seize and confine it. Since the beginning of recorded time, powerful rulers have created zoological gardens or menageries. Owning exotic animals was a sure way to show off wealth and secure stature, and the more dangerous your animals, the more daring and dramatic your mastery over nature.

Captive pigeons were kept as early as 4500 B.C. in what is now Iraq. Two thousand years later, men were taming elephants in India. Around 1490 B.C., Egypt's Queen Hatshepsut spon-

Us Against Them

In Greek mythology, after a phase of violent warfare among the gods when all mortal life perished, Zeus gave the Titan Prometheus and his brother Epimetheus the task of repopulating the earth. He left them with gifts to divvy up, and the brothers got to work crafting man and beast of river clay. Prometheus painstakingly modeled humans after the gods, while the more impulsive (and arguably imaginative) Epimetheus, whose name means "he who thinks after," cranked out creature after creature—furred, fanged, finned, and each more fabulous than the last—and quickly lavished on them Zeus's valuable gifts. And so these varied creatures got warm fur coats and feathers, protective spines and armor, keen senses, speed, strength, and cunning, while vulnerable humans were left to shiver through the terrors of night.

Fond of his own wretched creation, Prometheus stole fire from the gods to sustain it. He was severely punished for this and other crimes of compassion on behalf of humankind, and he was chained to a mountaintop, where every day an eagle—an agent of the other kingdom—swooped from the sky to feast on his liver. Every night the liver grew back again, and Prometheus suffered anew.

sored the first animal-collecting expedition on record, which brought back leopards, greyhounds, monkeys, and exotic birds. From then on, pharaohs and queens traditionally sponsored expeditions to bring back exotic creatures from faraway lands.

Almost every palace park kept a menagerie for the private pleasure of the court and foreign diplomats, and many of its animals were embalmed after they died. During royal processionals, hundreds of wild creatures might blur past among flashing gold and fluttering banners as the crowd looked on, and the public was allowed to toss cakes and scraps of meat to the sacred crocodiles of Lake Moeris or watch lions devour live prey at the Temple of the Sun in Metropolis.

Around 1100 B.C., King Wen of China created Ling-Yu, or the Garden of Intelligence. Established 800 years before the Great Wall, this vast 1,500-acre preserve between Beijing and Nanjing housed deer, antelope, goats, pheasants, and fish. It may have been used as a hunting park but was probably also deemed sacred, since people believed animals could trigger communication between the human and spirit worlds.

The business of collecting exotic creatures was likewise brisk in ancient Rome, though its ends were savage. In legend, at least, Egypt's Ramses II battled nobly alongside his favorite pet lion, Antam-nekt, but Nero—the Roman emperor most infamous for his cruelty—is said to have dined with Phoebe, his pet tiger, who feasted in turn on unloved or otherwise expendable houseguests.

Romans might enjoy up to 175 days of festivals and celebrations a year, seated with hundreds of thousands of others in vast, roofless amphitheaters or "circuses." Here they watched thunderous chariot races and gory mortal contests between gladiators. Bulls, deer, and elephants mauled one another or perished at the point of Roman spears and swords, while horsemen squared off against hundreds of bears and lions. The Romans even filled amphitheaters with water to stage hippo fights. Sources have it that in a single day, when Titus inaugurated the Colosseum in A.D. 80, anywhere from 5,000 to 9,000 animals were killed.

Constantine, the first Christian emperor of the Roman Empire, temporarily banned such blood sport, but by the sixth century Justinian had brought the games back. In some places they kept up even after the fall of the Roman Empire, into the twelfth century.

Every emperor had a zoological collection, or menagerie, to support such occasions. Nero kept some 400 bears; Trajan, 11,000 animals of every known species; Augustus, 420 tigers.

The Romans also used animals for ceremonial purposes. Beginning with Augustus, it was the custom for emperors to travel in a chariot pulled by four elephants during victory parades. Ceremonial elephants marched in circles at official events, scattering flowers among onlookers. Trained to withstand crowds, these creatures had their mild manners tested by keepers who crept up and blew

bugles or clapped cymbals behind them during solemn processions.

In contrast, Roman war elephants were trained to tread enemy soldiers and hurl heavy arrows with their trunks. They could wreak havoc in the right battle, but as armies in India and Southeast Asia had already discovered, elephants were unreliable weapons; they could easily panic and trample their own troops as well as the enemy's.

By the fourth century B.C., most Greek city-states had menageries, but the Greeks were as concerned with nature as a science as they were with displaying wealth and power. They opened the first public zoos as centers for study and experimentation, and in the time of the philosopher Aristotle—student of Plato and teacher of Alexander the Great—young scholars would have been regularly exposed to monkeys and talking parrots as part of their education. Alexander often gets credit for creating the first public zoo (perhaps because it was in Alexandria), but in fact his successor, Ptolemy I, built it. Ptolemy II continued the work, and under his reign this collection became one of the most impressive in the world.

Alexander brought back elephants and other animals as the spoils of war, and he was granted still others, a tiger among them, in tribute. His famous teacher surely got to observe and record them, one and all, for his zoological encyclopedia, *History of Animals.* People in those days discovered the wider world through the works of natural philosophers like Aristotle or historians like Herodotus, who in turn often gathered their data from travelers, soldiers, and hunters. Some reports were more fanciful than others, depicting creatures and behaviors both spectacular and terrifying: glowing birds that lit a traveler's way through the forest at night; massive dog-size ants that unearthed gold with their claws; and the merciless man-eating manticore, a lion with a scorpion's tail and the face of a human. People read these accounts eagerly and believed them. They invented fables about the beasts and illustrated maps with their images.

Early naturalists, such as the Roman writer Pliny, who died while observing firsthand the eruption of Mount Vesuvius, collected and spread fascinating and sometimes equally fanciful "facts" about animal behavior. Of elephants, for instance, who display "honesty, wisdom, justice, [and] also respect for the stars and reverence for the sun and moon," Pliny gives this tender secondhand account: "In the forests of Mauritania, when the new moon is shining, herds of elephants go down to a river named Amilo and there perform a ritual of purification, sprinkling themselves with water, and after thus paying their respects to the moon return to the woods carrying before them those of their calves who are tired." What's more, writes Pliny, elephants "homage their king by kneeling before him and proffering garlands."

This type of moral view of animals and the natural world is famously evident in the tales of the legendary Greek fabulist and slave Aesop, which are less about the real animals that inhabit them than the morals they extol: "appearances are deceptive," "one good turn deserves another," or "slow and steady wins the race."

Hannibal at the Gate

In one of the boldest military campaigns of the Second Punic War—and perhaps of all time—the Carthaginian commander Hannibal set out from Spain circa 218 B.C. to mount a surprise attack on Rome. With an army of about 50,000 men and 37 elephants, including his own Indian elephant, Surus, Hannibal traversed some 1,500 miles of hostile territory. After successfully crossing the Pyrenees mountains, his force encountered the surging Rhone, its banks thick with enemy soldiers. Hannibal's men built huge rafts, spread dirt over them to simulate solid ground, and lured the anxious elephants aloft, towing them over the river to safety. But now for the most famous and daring aspect of Hannibal's campaign: he led his army of foot soldiers, cavalry, pack animals, and subtropical elephants over the mighty Alps in November.

It was a perilous fifteen-day crossing—fierce mountain tribes showered them with stones, and men and pack animals tumbled from the icy, steep passes—during which Hannibal lost a huge share of his troops, but he somehow managed to get all 37 elephants across alive and into Italy, where they promptly repaid the favor by crushing the Roman

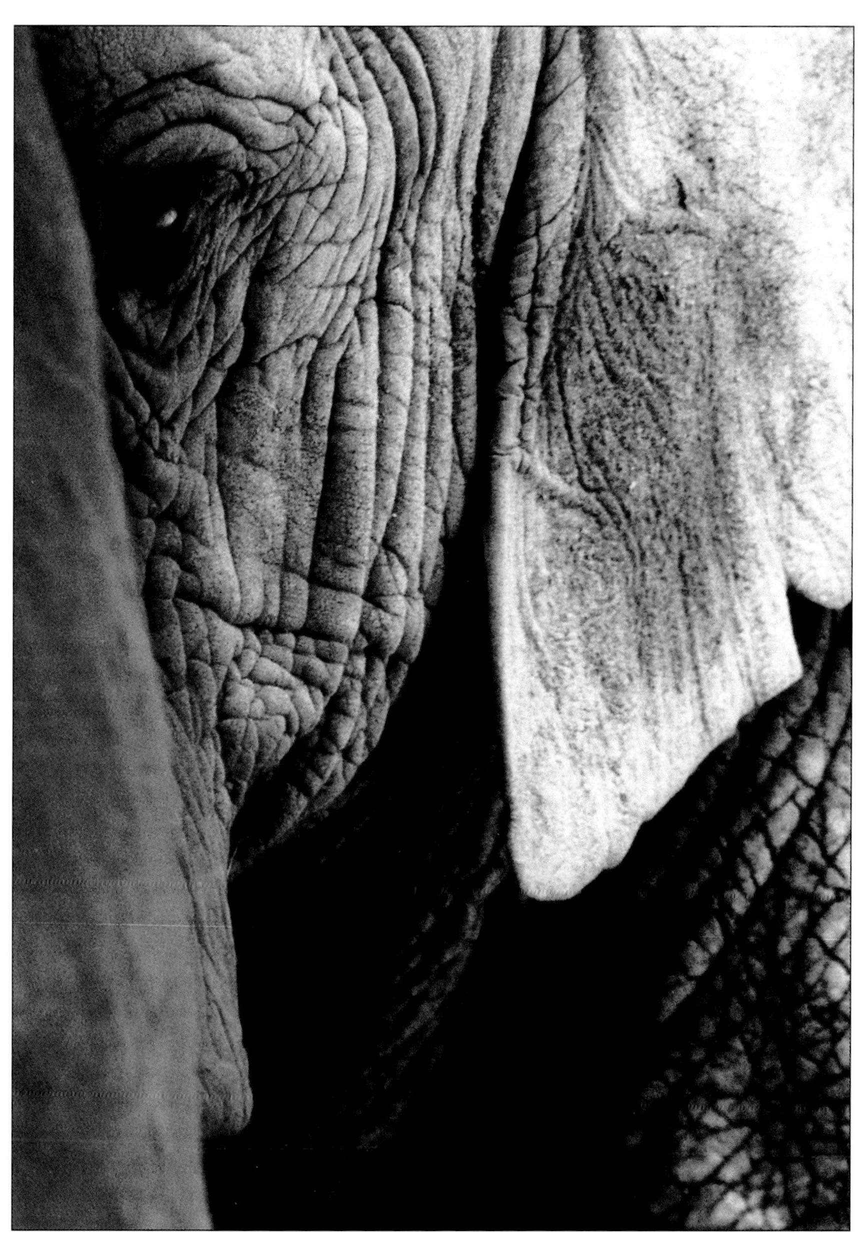

The Peacock and the Crane

A Peacock spreading its gorgeous tail mocked a Crane that passed by, ridiculing the ashen hue of its plumage and saying, "I am robed, like a king, in gold and purple and all the colors of the rainbow; while you have not a bit of color on your wings."

"True," replied the Crane. "But I soar to the heights of Heaven and lift up my voice to the stars, while you walk below, like a cock, among the birds of the dunghill."

Fine feathers don't make fine birds.

Pet Familiars and Pigs on Trial: Crime, Punishment, and Spectacle in the Middle Ages

For centuries—well into the Middle Ages—people continued to rely for their understanding of the natural world on the recorded wisdom of ancient observers like Pliny and Aristotle. Much of this wisdom trickled down into the medieval bestiary, a collection of inherited, usually unverified zoological observations of animals matched with fanciful illustrations. Generations of scribes copied out the text, adding or embellishing a little along the way, each contributing something new. Because the bestiary was popular reading in the Middle Ages, the church eventually used this entertaining and ever-evolving "book of beasts" to its advantage. As in *Aesop's Fables,* animals became instruments of moral and religious training.

The Book of Beasts

What sort of zoological "facts" might the curious reader encounter in a medieval bestiary?

- Elephants have no joints in their legs and are killed when mice crawl into their trunks, which lead directly to the brain.

- A female ape gives birth to twins: one it loves, and the other it hates. When pursued, the mother clutches her beloved in front while the despised offspring holds pitifully to her back.

- Bees are born from the corpses of cows.

- A bird called the Caladrius, kept in the king's house, will foretell the outcome of illness: If the bird does not gaze into the face of a sick man, that man will die. If the bird meets his eye, it will draw the ailment to itself and soar away into the sun, where the illness is consumed.

- If a man carries the heart of a male crow and a woman the heart of a female, they will agree between them all their lives.

- Weasels give birth through the mouth or ear.

- If you cut out the tongue of a live goose and lay it upon the breast of a sleeping person, he will confess all he has ever done.

➛ A jaculus, or flying serpent, lurks in trees until its prey blunders near, and then it hurls itself upon its victim.

➛ When two nightingales vie with one another in song, the loser dies, abandoning its life before its song.

➛ A hungry fox will roll in red mud to appear bloodstained, then lie still and let his tongue loll. When birds come to investigate the corpse, the fox springs to life again to feast.

➛ He who takes the heart of a stork, ties it up in the skin of a hawk, and writes upon it "because I have conquered mine enemies," next tying it to his right arm, will be invincible in war.

➛ Saint Hildegard of Bingen, in the twelfth century, advised, "Take some unicorn liver, grind it up and mash it with egg yolk to make an ointment. Every type of leprosy is healed, if treated frequently with this ointment."

Is it any wonder that people loved to read these fascinating accounts—if whimsical by today's scientific standards—at a time when the world was eager for evidence of God's wonders?

Most animal entertainments of the time were less enlightening and a good deal bloodier. As in ancient Rome, animal fighting or baiting was a popular pastime in medieval Britain and Europe, one that persisted well into the seventeenth century. King James liked to pit lions against dogs, bulls, and boars, and Queen Elizabeth I, visiting Kenilworth in 1575, enjoyed watching a pack of mastiffs bait thirteen bears. Many traditional blood sports, such as bull-fighting and cockfighting, flourished in these centuries.

A Steep Admission Fee

Can you imagine donating your pet dog or cat to the London Tower Menagerie . . . as lion food? Some people did just that to pay their way, once the zoo opened to the public. Today we invest in health insurance for our poodles. Our Persians enjoy gourmet cat food. In general, we treat our companion animals as beloved members of the family, but this wasn't always so, at least not in ordinary households.

For various, often practical reasons, less privileged people of the past had comparatively little sentimental attachment to animals. Caring for a pet in the Middle Ages could even be dangerous.

In Britain between the years 1560 and 1700, countless innocent people were condemned and executed for witchcraft, a crime that involved feeding or scheming with evil spirits. English law held that a familiar was a demon-companion that carried out a witch's ill will in exchange for food and protection. It might appear as a dog, rabbit, mouse, toad, hedgehog, weasel—even a lamb or a foal—but familiars also often took the form of cats.

Animals in medieval Europe were in fact held accountable for crimes. The legal process for animal trials was as follows: If the accused beast had spilled blood, it was tried by a secular, or nonreligious, court; otherwise, the church doled out punishment.

Secular animal trials, against the likes of goring bulls and unruly boars, were a blunt business, usually ending in swift execution. More than forty pigs were prosecuted for attacking humans (the charge was often murder, especially of children), and while the earliest case dates to the thirteenth century, records exist all the way up through the mid-1800s. Some prosecutors apparently tortured the animals on the rack to hasten a confession before decking them out in human clothes and summarily hanging them. Pigs were the most common offenders, but other "criminals"—from kicking mules and goring bulls to nippy dogs and a cat that had clawed a child's face—also saw their day in court. In seventeenth-century Russia, a goat was sentenced to a year in a Siberian prison camp for butting a child down the stairs. Its owner had to pay the crown one kopek a day to cover the goat's expenses.

The Persecuted

The medieval Christian church linked the cat with pagan religions. Cats came to be thought of as elusive and evil, capable of sucking the breath from a sleeping baby. Not only was it okay to be cruel to them, but it was applauded as a means of thwarting evil. On St. John's Day, people all over Europe forced cats into sacks and hurled them into bonfires, or they tied them together by the tail and looked on as the bewildered animals writhed and clawed to get loose.

Cats weren't the only creatures with a bad reputation. Many animals were known to be allies of Satan. The serpent had tempted Eve, of course. And should a snake slide down the throat of a farmer asleep in his field, the man would surely wake to find himself possessed by the devil. Pigs also suffered ill regard, maybe because Christ was said to have cured the insane by driving out the evil spirits that took refuge in them, herding the fugitive spirits into hogs.

The theme of animals being used to waylay evil or illness also occurs in many cultures. The word *scapegoat,* in the sense of someone punished for the misdeeds of others, was a biblical mistranslation of the Hebrew word *azazel* (a demon's name) as *ez ozel* ("the goat that departs"). The word appears in Leviticus 16:10 in reference to an ancient Hebrew practice for Yom Kippur, the Day of Atonement, when two goats were gathered; one was sacrificed to God while the other was "given" the people's sins, then released into the wilderness to carry the sins away.

In *The Golden Bough,* a classic study in world folklore, magic, and religion, Sir James Frazer writes, "When cholera rages among the Bhars, Mallans, and Kurmis of India, they take a goat or a buffalo—in either case the animal must be a female, and as black as possible—then having tied some grain, cloves, and a red lead in a yellow cloth on its back they turn it out of the village. The animal is conducted beyond the boundary and not allowed to return. Sometimes the buffalo is marked with a red pigment and driven to the next village, where he carries the plague with him." Frazer reports similar primitive practices in other parts of India, as well as in Egypt, Bolivia, and Peru.

The ecclesiastical animal trials were a still more peculiar business. Here an entire species of offending animal, often insects, might stand accused of infesting a village or parish. A senior church official or cleric acted as judge, and qualified attorneys handled the defense and prosecution. If convicted, the cleric vowed to excommunicate the group if it didn't retreat at once, which sounds absurd to modern ears, but medieval people placed great trust in bishops and church leaders and believed they could conjure demons, call forth rain, and divert storms.

Amazing though it may seem, these trials often gave a reasonable chance at justice, as they were conducted with all due ceremony. The accused might receive legal aid and be appointed a defense lawyer at taxpayers' expense. Both sides presented evidence and called witnesses.

In a famous 1587 trial in the French wine district of St. Julien, local crops were invaded by a species of greenish weevil. On April 13, the insects stood trial. Not only did the defense attorney get them off, but he got them reparations! If the weevils vacated the vineyards, the court agreed, compensation would follow in the form of an alternate parcel of land. When the weevils' lawyer objected that the relocation plot was substandard, court officials went to inspect the property, and so on. Eventually, after some tough negotiating, the parties reached a settlement.

The Pomp and Arrogance of Tyrants

In 1792, during the French Reign of Terror, when the royal and the rich were unpopular, to say the least, a parrot with the bad sense to blurt out, "Long live the king!" on a crowded Paris street was brought before the revolutionary tribunal. The bird and the two noblewomen who owned it wound up in a Parisian courtroom, where officials commanded the bird, accused of counterrevolutionary activities, to speak its piece. The parrot only whistled.

Like many rulers before him, Louis XVI of France viewed his treasured menagerie as a symbol of his power. But his was an age of sweeping change. Lands and wealth were being redistributed to the masses, and many people saw the royal animal collection at Versailles not as proud proof of political power, but as a symbol of oppression.

During the French Revolution, in October 1789, a mob is said to have stormed Versailles with the aim of freeing the animals in the king's menagerie. They came "in the name of the people and in the name of nature to order [the director] to liberate the beings that had emerged free from the hands of the Creator and had been unduly detained by the pomp and arrogance of tyrants." The director agreed but warned that captives with a taste for meat might have the bad manners to eat their liberators.

The revolutionaries settled for a partial release, and by about 1793 the rest of the royal menagerie had been transferred to Jardin des Plantes, blazing a way for what is often thought of as the scientific age of zoos.

People of the Middle Ages lived in close quarters with native and domestic animals, but the ordinary public had little chance to glimpse exotic wildlife as they once had in ancient Greece and Rome. Viewing foreign beasts, whether matched in combat or merely displayed, was a privilege for the privileged—reserved only for royalty and nobility.

Medieval folk labored most or all their lives in a single small community. There was little leisure time, and those who did find free time probably wouldn't—for lack of money, transportation, and decent roadways—spend it traveling. The average person likely saw fewer than one hundred people in a lifetime; so imagine the mood when wagons full of actors, jugglers, and bards rolled into the village. Often these traveling showmen had with them caged native animals—bears, bulls, badgers, wild boars, or marmots—and if you wanted blood sport, chances are you'd have it. But beginning late in the sixteenth century, such troupes were as likely to showcase dancing dogs or even apes.

The art of training animals, which the ancient Egyptians had developed and excelled at, and which was largely forgotten during the Middle Ages, made a comeback in the late sixteenth and seventeenth centuries. Performing animals were a common sight at English fairs and markets of the time. In London, handbills advertised Russian flea circuses, feline operas, vaulting apes, drumming hares, and domino-playing dogs. Throughout the 1590s you could even visit London Bridge for a peek at Mr. Holden's Dancing Camel.

"It is a rule in the nature of horses, that they have an especiall regard to the eye, face, and countenaunce of their keepers."

—William Banks

A Horse of Strange Qualities

In the mid-1590s, an Englishman named William Banks and his horse, Maracco, were among London's most renowned entertainers. Eventually their fame would spread throughout the British Isles and into Europe, even rating mention in Sir Walter Raleigh's *History of the World* and William Shakespeare's play *Love's Labour's Lost.*

Maracco wore silver shoes and could count by stamping his hoof, prance forward or backward on two legs, dance, kneel, scamper, hold his hooves straight out in front of him, and play dead with flair. He could locate a man with spectacles in a crowd of 200, bow in honor of the queen, and deliver a glove to a lady spectator with a green or purple or crimson muff.

One day in February of 1601, Banks led his horse up a spiral staircase with some thousand steps and out onto the roof of St. Paul's Cathedral. Here, 520 feet above London streets alive with gaping jugglers, peddlers, strolling nobles, and beggars, Maracco danced and did tricks. The real wonder is how Banks got the horse down again, but he did, and not long after, the celebrated pair set off for an extended tour of the Continent.

Superstition and accusations of witchcraft were very much a part of life in those days, and many who saw Mr. Banks and his "Horse of Strange Qualities" must have suspected black magic. In Paris, however, a city magistrate took action: he put horse and master in jail for questioning. Banks managed to convince his interrogators that the horse's tricks were a result of careful training, and he and Maracco were released.

But the next year, they frightened an audience in Orléans, which grew agitated and insisted Banks must be a sorcerer and his horse a demon. Again the two were arrested, but this time their captors threatened to burn them alive. Mr. Banks requested and secured the right to stage a farewell performance for the accusing priest and monks. Banks instructed Maracco to single out the priest with a crucifix in his hat. Maracco obeyed and, kneeling before the symbol, seemed to kiss it devoutly. His accusers then had to admit their error, as everyone knew the devil couldn't approach the cross. Maracco, it seemed, had been moved by the Holy Ghost.

William Banks never revealed specific training secrets, but from the time Maracco was a foal, he said, he'd spent the better part of every day with him, forging a bond. He let no one else feed or pat the horse and, depending on Maracco's performance during a session, either rewarded the horse with kindness and loaves of bread or withheld food as needed to discourage willfulness.

Modern show and circus horses do everything from walk on stilts to dive from high platforms into massive tubs of water—but you probably won't find a trick to top the one on St. Paul's Cathedral.

Not surprisingly, the world's ruling classes have been consistent and indulgent pet owners.

The seventeenth-century Japanese Shogun Tsunayoshi, sometimes called the Dog Shogun, at one point cared for 100,000 dogs. The expense triggered national inflation and a much-resented tax on farmers.

Lap dogs were especially popular with the aristocracy. Mary Stuart, or Mary Queen of Scots, was rarely without an entourage of little dogs and had them dressed in blue velvet suits to keep warm in winter. Eyewitness accounts of the queen's last moments tell how one of her executioners, "pulling off her garters, espied her little dogge, which was crept under her clothes, which could not be gotten forth but by force, yet afterwards would not departe from the dead corpse but came and lay between her head and her shoulders."

Mary Stuart launched generations of dog-loving monarchs: James I, Charles I, Charles II, and James II were all devoted dog owners. The Stuarts' public passion for dogs may have provided an early model for the less privileged and fashionable. As revolution, democracy, trade, and industry began to reshape society in ensuing centuries—and a new, urban middle class emerged—attitudes about animals changed, too, and by the nineteenth century many ordinary people had discovered the rewards of pet keeping. French dog-care books of the day proposed elegant outfits for companion animals—everything from dressing gowns and traveling cloaks to rubber boots, silver collars, and designer kennels. Dogs in fashionable middle-class Parisian families wore outfits coordinated with their mistresses' and were in general washed, primped, perfumed, and powdered.

The little spaniels now named for Charles II had full run of the palace while he reigned, inspiring one courtier to quip, "God save your Majesty, but god damn your dogs."

Devil Cats and Machines: The Age of Exploration

The wonders of the wider world were becoming more accessible all the time, as methods of travel improved and more and more people took to the roadways and high seas. Near the end of the fifteenth century, the race to find the quickest route to fabled Asia inspired an Age of Exploration that led to European colonization of the New World. People, diseases, plants, and animals crisscrossed oceans, mixed and mingled, and forever altered native landscapes.

Whether driven across oceans by the lure of silk, spices, and untold wealth or by the urge to spread Christian gospel and escape religious persecution, people found that faster and sturdier ships—plus improvements in mapmaking, navigation, and naval artillery—made the quest for glory, gold, and God not only possible but imperative in an age when nations and empires were competing for global prominence. Meanwhile, Europeans brought horses, cattle, turnips, sugar, and smallpox to the Americas. Potatoes, tomatoes, maize, tobacco, and syphilis circled back to Europe. Formerly isolated cultures or ecosystems adapted or were decimated.

In 1519, the Spanish explorer Hernando Cortés entered Tenochtitlán, the Aztec capital, and stumbled across one of the most extraordinary zoos anyone had ever seen. Looming behind Montezuma's palace, the collection was so vast it took hundreds of keepers to care for it. Captive eagles and hawks devoured five hundred turkeys a day. And beyond aviaries and ponds full of birds, beyond vast tanks of fish and snake enclosures, the visitor encountered pacing pumas and jaguars, sloths, monkeys, and armadillos behind bronze bars.

Cortés attacked in 1521 and ultimately obliterated the city, but some of the 300,000 residents are said to have survived for a time by eating the animals in Montezuma's menagerie.

In general, Christian attitudes of the time toward the animal kingdom—as distinct from the "Kingdom of Man"—might be summed up in the first chapter of Genesis: "God blessed them, and God said unto them, Be fruitful, and multiply, and replenish the earth, and subdue it; and have dominion over the fish of the sea, and over the fowl of the air, and over every living thing that moveth upon the earth." In other words, we're boss, and animals are here to serve our needs.

For many Christian Europeans in the sixteenth and seventeenth centuries, wild nature was not only a symbol of chaos but the devil's playground. In their sermons, Reverend Cotton Mather and other New England Puritans spoke of the wilder-

The Ghost in the Machine

Even after the rise of rational scientific thought, we held fast to our distinctly human advantage. "I think, therefore I am," proposed René Descartes, a French philosopher and mathematician who lived and wrote in the first half of the seventeenth century. Without a human soul and consciousness—"the ghost in the machine"— animals were just machines built of flesh. This Cartesian or "mechanistic" philosophy made it okay to subject animals to brutal medical experiments, but those very experiments revealed how similar the physiologies of other vertebrates (animals with backbones) are to our own, in some cases almost identical!

The philosopher Voltaire challenged Descartes outright: "Answer me, mechanist, has Nature arranged all the springs of feeling in this animal to the end that he might not feel?" It would be interesting to hear how Descartes responded. It's also worth noting that the influential thinker kept a pet dog. I can't help imagining him at his ease by the evening fire, absently stroking the head of the little animal he called "Monsieur Grat." Did Descartes really look down and see just a machine?

ness as an insult to God. To civilize the New World "savages" and the land they inhabited was to vanquish evil, and settlers cleared forests and drained marshes for moral as much as economic reasons.

The New World pioneer was a hero who mastered the wild—or obliterated it—and predators were especially maligned. The gray wolf was so plentiful at the time that contemporaries like William Wood lamented, "There is little hope of their utter destruction, the Countrey being so spacious, and they so numerous, travelling in the Swamps by Kennels: sometimes ten to twelve are of a company. Late at night, and early in the morning, they set up their howlings [what another writer of the time called "dismal howlings"] and call their companies together, at night to hunt, at morning to sleepe; in a word, they may be the greatest inconvenience the Countrey hath." In 1630, leaders of the Massachusetts Bay Colony offered a wolf bounty of a penny a head. Other colonies followed suit, and by 1800 New England and eastern Canada had more or less achieved the "utter destruction" of the gray wolf.

Like the wolf, the cougar was a competitor for game in the New World and a threat to livestock. Cougars stalked through American folklore, slinking down from the mountains to appear out of nowhere with a hair-raising scream. Their guarded nature surely fed their fabled status as "devil cats." As early as the 1500s, Jesuit priests in southern California were rewarding Native Americans with a bull for every cougar killed, and in 1674, Connecticut offered a bounty of twenty shillings per cat.

By 1803, President Thomas Jefferson sent Captain Meriwether Lewis, Captain William Clark, and the men who made up their Corps of Discovery on an 8,000-mile round-trip journey across the American West to map territory acquired from France and find a trade route to the Pacific Ocean. But Jefferson also craved word of "the animals of the country generally, and especially those . . . which may [be] deemed rare." The expedition ultimately noted and described the habits and habitats of some 122 new animals.

Journals from the expedition recall a landscape teeming with life. Just 200 years ago many thousands of migrating bison shook the open plains. Massive flocks of pigeons blotted out the sun. Salmon clogged the Columbia River to such a degree that it seemed you could scale their backs to get from one bank to the other.

But as settlers, fur trappers, and others spread west across the rivers, plains, and mountains, they exploited the land season after season—sometimes leaving wanton carnage in their wake. By 1892, the historian and author of *The California and Oregon Trail,* Francis Parkman observed:

> The sons of civilization, drawn by the fascination of a fresher and bolder life, thronged to the western wilds in multitudes which blighted the charm that had lured them. . . . The buffalo is gone, and of all of his millions, nothing is left but bones. . . . Those discordant serenaders, the wolves that howled at evening about the traveller's camp-fire, have succumbed to arsenic and hushed their savage music. . . . The rattlesnakes have grown bashful and retiring. The mountain lion shrinks from the face of man, and even grim "Old Ephraim," the grizzly bear, seeks the seclusion of his dens and caverns.

Sons of civilization had labored to control and confine the wild since ancient times, but the wholesale taming of the New World in these centuries—a campaign as efficient as it was reckless—must have led others besides Parkman to question the pace of discovery and destruction.

Elephant Martyrs and Ancestor Apes: The Victorians

Back in Europe, the royal and the rich continued to covet and collect wild animals zealously from the sixteenth through eighteenth centuries, although the word *zoo* wasn't formally used until the mid-nineteenth century. Humans also continued to use exotic animals as political barter to bribe, to apologize for shortcomings, and to pay tribute to or otherwise flatter and impress Very Important People.

Meanwhile, public menageries and traveling circuses became increasingly popular in England in the 1800s.

After a brief career on the London stage, a young Indian elephant named Chunee made a name for himself at the Exeter Change menagerie, where animals were packed into small cages in the apartments of a commercial building. Here Chunee consumed more than 800 pounds of hay, corn, straw, carrots, and biscuits a day and became a star, attracting luminaries like Princess Victoria, Lord Byron, and Charles Dickens.

But the star's fortunes took a turn for the worse one year when he entered musth—a state of surging testosterone that affects healthy adult bull elephants, usually in springtime, triggering furious tempers—and proceeded to gore the walls of his den, leaving the floor coated in plaster and mortar. Before long, Chunee had cracked a wooden beam and ripped down sections of the roof.

Sure that the five-ton beast would escape and release his wrath on an unsuspecting public—not to mention lions, tigers, and crocodiles—Chunee's keepers determined to put him down. They chose poison for their method and applied it to his food. Chunee refused it . . . time and again. His executioners enlisted a boy the elephant didn't know to slip him poison in a bun. Chunee eagerly consumed decoy buns the boy offered but trod the poisoned one underfoot. He understandably refused to eat after that, and instead went to work on another beam in his den, bringing down a rain of bricks and mortar, at which point spectators were evacuated from Exeter Change.

Those on hand armed themselves with cutlasses, bayonets, and harpoons as an eager mob—attracted by Chunee's enraged trumpeting and the answering roar of big cats—gathered outside the gates. Would the whole place come down? One keeper appealed to the Paddington police station, where patrolmen seized their truncheons and marched back to Exeter Change. The din of alarmed animals was "dreadful," according to one eyewitness, and keepers were scrambling to reinforce the broken bars on Chunee's den with rope as the elephant continued his rampage.

Rifle fire rained down on the enraged animal, but Chunee seemed unconquerable. More weaponry was sent for and distributed among the growing array of Exeter Change staff, policemen, and soldiers. The assembled fired some fifty rounds, and though Chunee fell to his knees with a groan at one point, he furiously reared up again to renew his attack. At length, one of his keepers commanded the elephant to kneel—as he so often did at showtime—and in a bittersweet act of obedience, Chunee did as he was told, but this time his keeper rewarded him with a bayonet in the flank. A man with a rifle crept close and fired at close range, and, after a final feverish lunge, Chunee fell dead, just as still more reinforcements arrived (with a cannon in tow!).

The unruly crowd forced its way inside, only to be struck dumb by the sight of the fallen giant. The doors of Exeter Change remained open till midnight, with gawkers and mourners flowing in to glimpse the elephant "in state" while Chunee's keepers pondered how to dispose of his not insubstantial remains.

Despite this bleak affair, Exeter Change flourished as a London institution for some years, but meanwhile poems and plays were composed in Chunee's honor. Engravings dramatized the noble giant's gory demise, and pamphlets and newspapers published sensational reports of "the martyred elephant." These accounts spotlighted Chunee's untimely death—but also his unfortunate life of hardship and maltreatment. Already, many people of enlightened scientific mind considered it cruel to confine large wild animals in cramped indoor cages, and Chunee's very public fate only hastened a view toward animal welfare.

The physical makeup of such western menageries hadn't advanced much by the turn of the nineteenth century. Enclosures were little more than boxes with metal bars, or pits in the ground, built with no thought for an animal's health and well-being. They were designed to give spectators a view and offered no place for animals to hide.

The Zoological Society of London established its collection in Regent's Park in 1828, and its mission—in stark contrast to the circus atmosphere of Exeter Change—helped define our modern concept of zoos: to "offer a collection of living animals . . . brought from every part of the globe to be applied either to some useful purpose or as objects of scientific research, not of vulgar admiration."

A Royal Menagerie

Though animals had been kept in the Tower of London since the reign of King John, the Royal Menagerie began in earnest with three leopards. The Holy Roman Emperor, Frederick II, gave them to his new brother-in-law, England's King Henry III, as a gift— probably with Henry's coat of arms in mind. A favorite emblem in heraldry, the lion (a ready symbol of royalty, bravery, and strength) appears on shields and coats of arms in fifteen different postures; Henry's crest boasted three. Frederick must have figured three leopards would be close enough.

The Tower Menagerie evolved over 600 years and at various times housed a rhinoceros, a giraffe, zebras, kangaroos, llamas, ostriches, alligators, and a brave spaniel that one of the Tower lions took to as a pet. During the realm of Henry III, the collection even boasted a polar bear. It's said the captive swam from a leash and fished each day for its dinner in the Thames River.

This new scholarly purpose, echoing the scientific perspective of the Jardin des Plantes in France, saw popular support at a time of rapid urban development. Together with the publication of Darwin's *On the Origin of the Species* in 1859, the growth of cities and industry fed the public's appreciation for a vanishing natural world, along with its hunger for scientific understanding and ordering of that world. Zoological societies formed. Zoological gardens were established, with the term *zoo* first appearing in print in 1847. Scientific knowledge was now the primary justification for animal displays, though "vulgar admiration" continued to lure a paying public.

For even the most educated Victorians, science and spectacle were hard to separate. No matter how edifying the experience of viewing animals, it was still about the thrill. People craved the satisfying illusion of human mastery over nature, and in an age of imperial conquest, the average sophisticated Londoner or Parisian viewing dangerous beasts from far corners of the globe could enjoy, in the process, a sense that society had subdued the remote places from which these creatures hailed.

As the century progressed, the telegraph and print media helped make zoos more accessible and popular, and more competitive. A successful zoo, many believed, should feature "one of each" (like a dutiful postage stamp collection). The more—and more exotic—the creatures in your collection, the more people flocked to see them. The press also glorified the exploits of the hunter-adventurers who supplied the beasts, adding another layer of showmanship to the science of zoo management.

Individual animals, especially those deemed exceptionally romantic or exotic, became celebrities. There was a public uproar when the showman P. T. Barnum purchased the elephant Jumbo from the London Zoo and made ready to ship his prize to America. The famed pachyderm was the pride of England, a favorite of Queen Victoria herself, and the loss of him was staggering—even scandalous. The editor of the British *Daily Telegraph* telegrammed Barnum in the interests of the nation:

> Editor's compliments. All British children distressed at elephant's departure. Hundreds of correspondents beg us to inquire on what terms you will kindly return Jumbo.

Barnum's reply?: "My compliments to Editor Daily Telegraph and British nation. Fifty millions of American citizens anxiously await Jumbo's arrival . . ."

ELUSIVE CAPTIVES

European scientific voyagers of the eighteenth and nineteenth centuries busily harvested animals from all around the world for study and profit. How the gemlike hummingbird—nearly impossible to capture alive—frustrated them! One lucky collector seized one when he happened to see it enter the funnel of a huge flower. Stealthily, he pinched the petals closed, snipped the stalk, and slapped bird-in-flower into a cage. Most everyone who chanced to glimpse the fabled bird, it seemed, wanted one.

The metabolism of hummingbirds is so high—in need of frequent feeding—that some species enter a low-energy-use state called torpor. If they don't slow their heartbeat and breathing to save energy, they risk starving to death in their sleep. Easy to see why such a creature, caged for the duration of a scientific expedition and bound to the whims of a ship's crew, would suffer at sea. Rarely did a captive live more than a few days. "Only dead ones have been brought to Europe," one voyager lamented, and by then "the brilliance of their magnificent plumage is considerably dulled." This fleeting creature—like a bewitched jewel that dissolves at the touch of human hands—eluded all who would possess it.

In an era before field photography, the great ornithologist and bird artist John James Audubon was likewise frustrated in his desire to copy Nature "in her own way, alive and moving." Live models moved, all right, too quickly for him to complete a sketch. Dead ones betrayed none of the spark he was after, and what's more, he wrote, "Neither wing, leg, nor tail could I place according to my wishes." So Audubon devised a method of using different lengths of wire to hold fresh-killed birds in lifelike attitudes.

Naturalists and others who study animals and animal behavior have always walked a hard road to knowledge. Not only do skins and other preserved artifacts—pried from the life force that animated them—fade, but captive animals are notorious for behaving other than they would in their natural habitats. Zoo behaviors such as overeating, oversleeping, rocking and head bobbing, eating and throwing feces, pacing endlessly, and regurgitating food are uncommon or unheard of in the wild; they're the products of captivity and present an altered picture of an animal and its habits.

Most animals have common names, like "beetle" or "crocodile," but there are usually many—sometimes a great many—species of each. Common names can also differ from language to language and from country to country. As people became more interested in taking a scientific approach to the natural world, they began to group and identify living things as a means of sorting them and making them easier to manage and discuss.

The system of classification used today is based on the work of the eighteenth-century Swedish botanist Carolus Linnaeus. Scientists classify living things into large groups called kingdoms, made up of organisms that share basic characteristics but also differ in ways. All animals survive, for instance, by eating either plant life or other animals, but not all animals have a digestive cavity.

The five kingdoms are Animals, Plants, Fungi, Protists, and Monerans, so as it turns out bird, beast, and boy all share the same broad scientific classification. Like moles and monkeys, humans reside squarely in the Animal Kingdom. So much for "us and them."

Of course, each kingdom in the Linnaeus system can be divided into smaller and smaller groups, including Subkingdom, Phylum, Class, Order, Family, Genus, and the smallest group, Species. The first Latin word in an animal or plant's "scientific" name, which is identifiable to scientists anywhere on the globe, stands for the genus the organism belongs to. The second is its species name. Members of the same species share the same general physical appearance and can reproduce together.

River otter, Lutra canadensis

• • •

Until the eighteenth century, most Christians believed that Earth was formed precisely as described in the Bible; it had been altered by dramatic events set in motion by God, like the great flood; and it was several thousand, not millions of years old. God fashioned the world's flora and fauna as reported in Genesis, and the natural world had remained constant ever since, with humans holding a seat of honor at the top of a great Chain of Being.

But certain theories and discoveries had begun to challenge the widely established view of creation. According to the new science of geology, for instance, Earth had changed gradually over millions of years, and was changing still. Scientists like Erasmus Darwin, grandfather of the famous naturalist Charles Darwin, had speculated that species adapted ever so slowly to their environments. If a trait—like a giraffe's long neck or a zebra's stripes—helped a species adapt, it would be passed down to the next generation; if it didn't, it would gradually disappear.

Between 1831 and 1836, the research vessel *Beagle* set out to survey the South American coast, stopping in the Galápagos Islands on the equator, near Ecuador. The young Charles Darwin, serving as ship's naturalist, encountered numerous species of tortoise on these volcanic islands and collected many varieties of finch. Back home in London, he and the ornithologist John Gould cataloged and studied the birds, noting that some

Each zebra has its own identifying pattern of stripes,

much like our individual fingerprints.

In a large group, the stripes break up their outline and confuse predators.

plies in coastal caves. They found a fast source of fresh meat in meandering 400-pound tortoises, and soon every ship crossing the southern Pacific Ocean was weighing anchor in the Galápagos. Tortoises can go months without food or water, so whalers, merchants, and naval officers hauled them in by the thousands and kept them aboard as insurance against hunger. At the same time they left behind a deadly stowaway: the black rat, which went to work on tortoise eggs. As people settled the islands, domestic cats, dogs, and pigs joined the feast, devouring eggs and young, and trampling tortoise nests.

By the 1900s, scientists could see that several species would soon be extinct, but it wasn't until 1959 that Ecuador declared the Galápagos Islands a wildlife sanctuary and national park. It may be too late for George and his kind, but thanks to vigilant protection, other tortoise species on the Galápagos are flourishing today.

Galápagos tortoise

finches had beaks ideal for snatching insects or sipping nectar, while others had short, blunt beaks right for splitting seeds. Darwin pondered this, concluding that all thirteen varieties (known today as "Darwin's finches") had developed from a single species. He would later use these observations to support his revolutionary theory of evolution by natural selection.

In his *On the Origin of the Species,* Darwin wrote: "Can we doubt (remembering that many more individuals are produced than can possibly survive) that individuals having any advantage, however slight, over others, would have the best chance of surviving and procreating their kind?" Species evolve by changing over generations to suit particular ways of life, he said. Eventually they become so distinct from their ancestors that they form a brand-new species. This theory of "natural selection" was radical enough, but Darwin's voyages and observations convinced him that all organisms were directly related to previously existing forms of life, and so to each other. Darwin was so unsettled by his emerging ideas about evolution and "common descent" that he did not go public with his findings

> Is man an ape or an angel?
>
> Now I am on the side of the angels.
>
> —Benjamin Disraeli, British statesman and author
>
> November 25, 1864

for twenty years. In an 1844 letter, he hinted at the revolutionary nature of his insights: "I am almost convinced (quite contrary to opinion [*sic*] I started with) that species are not (it is like confessing a murder) immutable."

All the same, in his 1871 book, *The Descent of Man,* Darwin proposed that humans had evolved from apelike ancestors in Africa.

His theories shocked and enraged many people. They challenged Christian ideals—and still do, in the framework of some faiths—by undermining a literal reading of biblical creation. And if human intelligence evolved from traits already present in animals, how could we be unique "higher" beings created in God's image? Darwin's ideas were, for some, a scandalous attack on everything sacred, but their influence has been immeasurable, inspiring a whole new field of scientific inquiry: evolutionary biology.

Clever Horses and Signing Chimps

At the turn of the twentieth century, a man named Wilhelm von Osten claimed he had taught a horse to do arithmetic. When von Osten scrawled "3 x 3" on a card and displayed it to Hans, the horse tapped a front hoof nine times. When von Osten wrote "2 + 4," Hans tapped out six. Even when quizzed by someone other than von Osten, Hans usually arrived at the answer, and his "cleverness" made him famous.

In 1904, Hans aced a round of demanding tests presented by Carl Stumpf, director of the Berlin Psychological Institute, and a panel of thirteen scientists. Unable to discredit the horse, the Hans Commission turned the study over to the psychologist Oskar Pfungst, who eventually proved that Hans was clever indeed, just not in the way everyone had hoped. He was, it turns out, reacting to minute physical cues from his trainer or test administrators, some as subtle as a flared nostril, and the fact that he had unwittingly duped the distinguished panel left many sensible people blushing.

A few years after this incident, the behaviorist school of psychology formed. Its advocates took issue with another controversial idea of Darwin's (formulated together with his colleague George Romanes): that differences in intelligence and emotion between humans and other animals are differences of degree and not kind. The evidence Darwin used, proponents claimed, was "anecdotal" (reports based on random incidents).

For the behaviorists, only observable behavior could be trusted. We might sense or suppose that animals think and feel, but where's the proof? Laboratory testing, behaviorists proposed, was the cure for uncertainty. Animals respond to stimuli. Animals *behave,* and only behavior can be objectively studied and confirmed through repetition. This way of thinking caught on, and more "anecdotal" or "anthropomorphic" methods were seen to undermine clearheaded principles of scientific investigation.

Clever Hans cast an embarrassing shadow over the fields of animal study, one that lingers today. What can field researchers draw from if not their own observations and experiences with individual animals? How many "anecdotes" make up a scientific pattern, and at what point do patterns add up to proof? The very traits that assure the integrity of scientific method—skepticism, material evidence, steadfast corroboration—can make progress appear plodding to the uninitiated. But every now and then, a startling insight will challenge established ideas and inspire a fresh angle of vision.

In 1960, at her research compound at Gombe, near Lake Tanganyika, Jane Goodall watched a chimpanzee trim a blade of grass, then poke it into a termite mound to tease out lunch. This behavior turned out to be widespread: chimps not only *used* tools, but made them. At the time, tool and language use were considered strictly human behaviors. Like Descartes' "ghost in the machine," they were our unique birthright, abilities that set us apart from other animals.

Jane Goodall's mentor, the paleontologist Louis Leakey, responded to her news with a famous telegram: "Now we must redefine tool, redefine Man, or accept chimpanzees as human."

Studies since have revealed that common chimpanzees are far from the cute, tame creatures depicted in the media. The most social of apes, they form large, complex communities of twenty to one hundred individuals and are well adapted to both forest and savannah. Clever and powerful, they wage war on their own kind and collaborate in the hunt. Male chimpanzees work together to stalk monkeys in trees. Some wait in ambush while others drive the monkey on to be battered or bitten to death. When chimps glimpse a leopard, they sound a loud alarm call that mobilizes the group. Together, they may drive off the prowler with sticks and stones.

Like humans, chimpanzees are engineers, adept at choosing, making, and adapting tools to a given end. They plan ahead and

can concentrate on a task for hours. Chimps have been seen using twigs to pry food from their teeth or ease *out* a rotting tooth. As Jane Goodall observed, East African chimps use peeled twigs or palm fronds to hook termites out of mounds and employ wads of leaves to sop up rainwater collected in tree holes. Their West African relatives use stones as hammers to split hard-shelled nuts.

For many, discoveries and distinctions like these have called into question the very notion of confining or using apes as laboratory subjects at all—but the behaviorist influence has been vast. Many scientists who work with animals still dread committing the sin of anthropomorphism. Some attribute emotion or intellect to nonhumans only grudgingly. Animals are *stressed,* not *sad, anxious,* or *mournful—aggressive,* not *angry*. They exhibit courtship, parental, or flight behaviors—not affection, love, or fear. "Anecdotal" evidence of the unusual skills or braininess of individual animals might impress the general public, but for much of the scientific community (no matter their level of affection or fascination for their subjects) the feats of a remarkable few are inconclusive.

Most thoughtful animal lovers take for granted that animals are emotionally and intellectually complex—though it may be near impossible to measure—just as we are, but proving it remains the puzzle. Our quest to know our animal fellows has inspired both misunderstandings and many novel attempts to communicate across species' lines.

In 1961, scientists opened the space capsule of a U.S. Mercury rocket on a three-year-old chimpanzee named Ham, fresh from his stint as the first primate in space and sporting a toothy grin. The crowd cheered. Flashbulbs flared and newspapers around the world printed photos of heroic Ham together with celebratory headlines. But Ham wasn't smiling to mark a successful flight. He was probably scared to death. His "smile" was the

What's in a Smile?

Capuchin monkeys—patient, companionable, and easy to train—sometimes help paraplegics and others with severe physical disabilities in the way that Seeing Eye dogs aid the blind. For a match to succeed, though, the human partner must understand monkey etiquette. For the capuchin, teeth are a weapon. Bared teeth are a threat. So when human admirers crowd around, smiling and laughing, the object of their delight may be bristling against perceived aggression. And even a well-trained monkey will bite under the wrong circumstances. It's natural to suppose that because we feel great when we smile and show our teeth, other animals—our primate relatives in particular—do, too.

chimpanzee's fear grin. Chimps have loose, flexible lips and communicate using many facial expressions and sounds. For Ham, a "play face" would have been a wide-open mouth with concealed lips and teeth, while pursed lips would probably convey anger.

When it comes to communicating with other species, we're hampered by assumptions, wishful thinking, anthropomorphism, and the very fact that human language is our chief means of defining and sharing our world.

But who can blame us for trying?

Scientists haven't yet identified any natural use of—or for—language in the wild, but studies suggest that all great-ape species can learn one. A chimpanzee named Washoe was the first nonhuman to master elements of American Sign Language (ASL).

Though we share some 96 percent of our DNA with chimps, our fellow primates will probably never speak to us outright; they have different vocal cords than we do. With this in mind—and the fact that chimps use gesture to communicate in spontaneous and flexible ways—Allen and Beatrice Gardner set out to teach Washoe ASL in 1967. The project was controversial. Skeptics granted that Washoe had learned signs, made requests, and followed instructions in ASL, but they challenged claims that she combined ASL signs in innovative ways or tried to teach ASL to another chimp. Washoe's signs were impoverished by human standards, these critics argued, and her behaviors could have been produced by the sort of operant conditioning techniques many animal trainers use.

In operant conditioning, an animal learns she can "produce a desired stimulus," or get what she wants—food, for instance—by behaving a certain way. When you reward or "positively reinforce" an animal for doing something, chances are good that the animal will do it again. Was Washoe really using language? Or just repeating a performance to earn rewards?

As a California graduate student in 1972, Dr. Francine Patterson began teaching ASL to a young female lowland gorilla named Koko. Project Koko is one of the world's longest ongoing interspecies communications projects, and observers say

Koko has advanced further than any other nonhuman. She speaks with her hands, making signs in succession to form short sentences, and her statements can range from three to six words. Koko has learned more than one thousand signs, comprehends some two thousand words of spoken English, initiates conversations with her human companions, and boasts an IQ of between 70 and 95 on a human scale where 100 is considered "normal." When she forgets a word or phrase, Koko has been known to invent one. When she couldn't find her Pinocchio doll, for instance, she asked for her "elephant baby." She called a mask "an eye hat," a ring, a "finger bracelet," and a lemon (Koko doesn't like lemons), "a dirty orange."

Koko was the first animal to tell humans how she felt, to tease and swap insults, and to set herself apart from humans by pronouncing herself a "fine animal gorilla." Researchers at Project Koko (also known as the Gorilla Language Project) argue that Koko has displayed, in less developed form, almost every aspect of human behavior, from humor and fantasy play to storytelling and moral judgment.

At the Language Resource Center in Georgia, meanwhile, scientists have taught bonobos—sometimes called pygmy chimpanzees—to communicate using a language of symbols and computer graphics. The bonobos understand spoken English but answer questions and ask for things by pointing to symbols standing in for words. A bonobo named Kanzi first learned to communicate this way, but other bonobos have excelled at it, learning hundreds of words and combining them to shape simple sentences.

The quest to communicate with other species isn't limited to primates. People have known since Aristotle's day that parrots talk back, and African Gray parrots are especially skilled mimics. But do they understand what they're "saying"? Irene Pepperberg's research with captive African Grays, including one famous parrot named Alex, suggests these birds can, to a degree, use human words in context. For example, when a fed-up researcher scolded the bird for some infraction and left the room, Alex called out, "Come here! I'm sorry!" He has a large vocabulary and draws on it with roughly the skill and sophistication of a two-year-old child. Alex can identify objects, shapes, and colors, acknowledge the concepts of same and different, and even boss around lab assistants to get what he wants.

The linguist Noam Chomsky once said that if apes *could* use language, they *would* use it in the wild; they don't, he argued, so they can't. There's an old phrase about achieving the unlikely or impossible "when pigs fly." Are we, in our efforts to teach other species language, trying to teach pigs to fly? And what's in it for them?

As operant conditioning and other animal training methods reveal, when something's on offer, when something's at stake, many species (and not just those we humans think of as unusually intelligent, like apes and dolphins) learn by leaps and bounds. Are these just mindless tricks, performed for a treat? Or are these animals consenting to an exchange triggered by incentive?

Do animals in the wild ever go out of their way to communicate with *us?* Well, there's one famous example: a bird called the honey guide. The nomadic Boran people of northern Kenya still harvest honey as their ancestors did, with a little help from this unique bird, which needs wax in its diet, notably beeswax, and has learned to enlist the help of humans. The bird makes a racket to gain a person's attention, flies off a short distance, then takes up its chattering again with its human partner in hot pursuit. Leading honey lovers up to a half mile away, it waits patiently for its host to tear open the exposed nest, extract the honey, and clear out. Then the clever bird feeds on the wax.

This example of animal-human communication-collaboration is tantalizing, but not terribly representative. With few exceptions, wild animals communicate with humans only by accident. Maybe, as a rule, they just don't need to talk to us, any more than pigs need to fly.

But we still long to speak with them.

"How many times I have wished that I could look out onto the world through the eyes, with the mind, of a chimpanzee," Jane Goodall has said. "One such minute would be worth a lifetime of research." Dr. Goodall is far from alone, but it will take many Kokos, many Alexes, before science can make up its collective mind about what animals can and can't, will and won't, do. And more scientists seem to be saying that it's fairer and more accurate to judge animals by the standards of their own species, instead of viewing them as not-so-successful humans—inferior models missing important parts, like the ability to master language. The number one goal in the natural world is survival, after all, and each species is uniquely suited to it, "smart" where it counts. Can chimp society benefit from an alphabet? Does computation help a horse be a better horse? Would a mother cowbird, which lays her eggs in another bird's nest, leaving them at the mercy of strangers, profit from a capacity for shame? If the goal is to impress human friends or observers . . . yes.

Animals have an amazing range of vocalizations. Frogs croak, crickets chirp, and birds sing. Mammals grunt, roar, and purr. And special microphones, machines that produce pictures of sound, and other technologies advanced after World War II have finally allowed us to tune in to less perceptible music: everything from the underwater clicks and booms of fish to shrimpy static and whales' songs; from the high-pitched calls of rats to the complex infrasonic rumbling that governs the lives of elephants. The other kingdom may or may not ever become fluent in *our* language, but—to our credit—we can learn to listen in anyway.

Part 2

Today and Tomorrow

Shape Shifting

In an essay called "The Long Loneliness," the naturalist and poet Loren Eiseley—in light of research then just publicizing the high native intelligence and communicative feats of bottle-nosed dolphins—proposed that it was for lack of hands (which our race uses to build, record history, and destroy) that dolphins might never demonstrate true intellectual kinship to humans.

"The Long Loneliness" was the first thing I ever read that asked the reader not to perceive an animal through the filter of human metaphor and imaginative reference, not to say: *a dolphin is like us in the following ways, and therefore worthy of our notice and applause,* but to make the opposite leap. To slip on the dolphin's skin and flippers, embrace its otherness, its unique perspective. "Let us try for a moment," Eiseley writes, "to enter the dolphin's kingdom and the dolphin's body, retaining, at the same time, our human intelligence." When we plunge, he concludes, "down into the deep waters as naked of possessions as when we entered life itself," what we discover is immediate and astonishing:

> No matter how well we communicate with our fellows through the water medium we will never build drowned empires in the coral, we will never inscribe on palace walls the victorious boasts of porpoise kings. We will know only water and the wastes of water beyond the power of man to describe. We will be secret visitors in hidden canyons beneath the mouths of torrential rivers. We will survey in astonishment the flotsam that pours from the veins of continents—dead men, great serpents, giant trees—or perhaps the little toy boat a child loosed far upstream. . . . Meaningless appearances and disappearances will comprise our philosophies. We will hear the earth's heart ticking in its thin volcanic shell. . . . Vapor, bird cries, and sea wrack will comprise our memories. We will see death in many forms and, on occasion, the slow majestic fall of battleships through the green light that comes from beyond our domain.

> Over all that region of wondrous beauty we will exercise no more control than the simplest mollusk. Even the octopus with flexible arms will build little shelters that we cannot imitate. Without hands we will have only the freedom to follow the untrammeled sea winds across the planet. . . . [Ours] will be a world not susceptible to experiment.

What a revelation, when first I read this. How preposterous of Eiseley to suggest that we be anything other than human in our view, and how visionary! He asks us outright to enter depths that are *not* human, that are as strange and compelling as the selkie's realm. And without our busy, capable hands, how would we fare there? How could we (would we?) impress ourselves, cast the light of our identity upon an already bedazzled world?

All of which, for me, begs the question: Would we do more for animals by learning to be less ourselves in relation to them? What happens when we try on *their* skins?

In folklore and in Hollywood, shape shifting invariably leads to trouble, unleashing malicious hybrids on an unwitting public. In the eastern Congo, a belief in human-leopard shape shifting was sometimes taken advantage of by Anioto, or "leopard men," who killed with clawlike weapons so their murders could be blamed on real leopards. While many Native American tribes celebrated the wolf as a successful predator and saw it as a spiritual ally, Navajo lore warns of human witches called skin walkers, who disguise themselves as wolves to engage their enemies or just engage in evil. And the werewolf—a human who assumes wolf form at the full moon to wreak destruction—figures prominently in European folklore.

But humans have a long history of more benign forms of shape shifting. South American Indians tell of shamans morphing into jaguars and jaguars into men. The Yanomamo Indians of Amazonian Venezuela believe the spirits of animals can communicate through humans, and during their ceremonies, elders take hallucinogenic drugs and invite animal spirits into their bodies. In North American Tlingit mythology, the animals were once people. Shocked and frightened when Raven released daylight from a box, they retreated to the woods and waters. In traditional Tlingit stories, humans and animals are relatives and can cross into each other's worlds.

Can ancient ideas about shape shifting aid modern science?

In myths and stories, humans who assume animal shape often end up acting, well, suspiciously human. Like the selkie's husband—who trapped the object of his affection in human form to hold her—we tend to anthropomorphize out of love, imposing human traits, dreams, wishes, and desires on the "other" to make that other more accessible, more like us, more likely to return our love. But in so doing, we miss the point: other species are *not* human. And by missing the point, what else are we missing?

Anthropomorphism defeats its own purpose: to know animals better. But on the other hand, as Albert Einstein famously said, "Imagination is more important than knowledge." Do we credit only what can be seen and verified? Or do we recognize and respect mystery, conceding all we don't know? Isn't it that humble impulse toward wonder that inspires us to investigate and corroborate in the first place?

We're only beginning to understand the complexities of animal behavior, but luckily a flair for shape shifting isn't confined to our ancient past or to traditional cultures. Modern science is full of expert and sensitive shape shifters, people who try, in Loren Eiseley's words, "to enter the dolphin's kingdom and the dolphin's body." Animal ethologists (who study animals in their natural environments), behavioral ecologists (who look at how animals adapt to different environments), conservationists, zool-

HOW DO THEY KNOW?

In December 2004, a tsunami set off by an earthquake in the Indian Ocean devastated Southeast Asia. Waves of up to fifteen feet wiped out whole towns and villages, demolished hotels, and killed more than 220,000 people. Shortly after the tragedy, Reuters news service ran a story titled "Where Are All the Dead Animals?" The report said Sri Lankan wildlife officials were bewildered. What could account for the fact that human losses had been so great along the island's coast, yet officials had no record of dead animals? The deputy director of the National Wildlife Department explained the phenomenon—like many have before him—by arguing that animals have a sixth sense, one that alerts them to danger. In some inexplicable way, they sense disaster before it strikes and flee.

Most people have stories of pets exhibiting uncanny behaviors: cats that know when it's time to go to the vet, even before the cat carrier comes out of the closet; horses that journey unfamiliar miles to find their way back to a stable; dogs that sense when their human companions are about to initiate a walk or arrive home. Documented instances abound of what seem to be animal telepathy or precognition, of animals "predicting" everything from earthquakes to epileptic seizures. How do they do it? Why do these phenomena—which seem to parallel such wild behaviors as migration and homing—defy scientific explanation?

ogists, psychologists, and others are hard at work the world over researching topics that call for varying degrees of animal empathy, for getting inside an animal's "skin" or senses.

Shape shifting is what imaginative scientists do every day.

People once believed that swallows survived winter, and so disappeared from view, by burrowing into the mud in the bottom of lakes. In time, scientists learned that what these birds actually do is fly all the way from Europe to Africa and back again every year. Which is stranger here or more remarkable—the truth, or the fiction?

Enter for a moment the mind and wingspan of an arctic tern. You're the size of a pigeon, but every year of your life (the average tern lives to be about twenty-five) you effectively circumnavigate the earth, pausing only briefly to rest on the waves. You migrate longer than any other bird, flying from your winter quarters in Antarctica to breed in the Arctic, and then you turn around and come back again. Roundtrip, you clock between 18,000 and 30,000 miles a year. In the course of a lifetime, you may cover *more than a million miles.*

Birds are probably our most famous migrants, since about half of some nine thousand species—from the arctic tern to the tiny ruby-throated hummingbird, which weighs just five grams but can cross the Gulf of Mexico without stopping—migrate annually, and many crisscross the globe. But hundreds of *billions* of individual animals, from wildebeest and salmon to bee and butterfly, are on the go on our planet at any given time. Compelled by instinct to feed or breed, they make perilous journeys that span inhospitable deserts, icy plains, and mountain ranges.

How do they do it? And what can we learn from it?

Some animals inherit a migratory route from their parents, a sort of map etched into their genes. Others maintain mental maps of land features like mountain ranges and coastline (if you're a dolphin, you memorize the shapes of the sea floor). Salmon rely on a powerful sense of smell to guide them back to the exact stream in which they were born. Starlings let the sun lead them, orienting themselves to its movements in the sky throughout the day. A loggerhead turtle finds its way by sensing the direction and strength of Earth's magnetic field, and mallard ducks navigate—like human sailors of old—by the stars in the night sky.

Scientists put what they learn through this kind of shape shifting—about migration and other animal behaviors—to all manner of economic, medical, and other practical uses. For instance, gulls, lapwings, and starlings are famous for ignoring scarecrows. They also tend to feed and nest near airfields and can be a real hazard to planes taking off or landing. An understanding of migration patterns helps here (a single bird can destroy a jet engine that costs $2 million, not to mention jeopardize human lives), but once you can predict which birds might take up residence, and when, what do you do about it?

Researchers have used raptors like eagles and falcons to help clear "pest" birds from airspace, exploiting the natural predator-prey relationship to a practical human end. People also record distinct species "scare" calls and strategically blast them around airfields, and this practice has helped cut down on bird strikes and risk to aircraft; similar efforts have been made to control crop damage by blaring scare calls from loudspeakers around cornfields and orchards. These broadcasts target a "pest" bird species by using its unique alarm call. So, in a way, we're talking to these birds in their language.

In the decades since Dr. Eiseley composed "The Long Loneliness," the U.S. Navy has been studying dolphins, beluga whales, sea lions, and other marine mammals, first to mimic how they move in the water—hoping to streamline torpedo and submarine designs—and eventually to aid navy divers, as marine

mammals can make continual deep dives without getting the bends, or decompression sickness. Bottle-nosed dolphins are especially dependable and easy to train. Their use of echolocation, or precise underwater sonar, is particularly helpful to recover exercise and training gear or locate sea mines and enemy divers before beating a swift and silent retreat.

Some human medicines or medical practices have similarly evolved from imitating other species. Many animals lick their own and other animals' wounds, keeping the area clean and providing salivary antibiotics. Monkeys have been seen using honey-like substances to treat wounds, while a chimp with a stomachache may ease her discomfort by feeding on a plant called aspilia. Chimps have also been known to put plant fibers and small sticks to work as dental floss and toothpicks or to help their peers pull loose "baby" teeth.

People in traditional cultures often watched the behavior of sick animals. If an animal displayed a certain symptom, then ate a certain plant and recovered, people with comparable symptoms tried it, too. The idea that we can make medical discoveries by watching animals even has a name, "zoopharmacognosy," from the Greek words *zoo, pharmakon,* and *gnosis,* which add up to "animal pharmaceutical knowledge."

Dogs and humans, of course, have a long cooperative history. In return for food and shelter, dogs have served as beasts of burden in war and peace, as guards, messengers, hunters,

herders, and finders of lost children. They've been our guides and companions for ages, but can shape shifting—"playing dog"—help us to help ourselves?

A British medical journal reported in 1989 that a Border collie–Doberman mix repeatedly nosed a mole on its owner's leg, even attempting to bite it off. Her pet's persistence led the woman to get the lesion examined, at which time she found out she had a malignant melanoma and entered treatment.

Both humans and dogs perceive scent through a membrane called the olfactory epithelium. Receptors topped with tiny hairs line this membrane, picking up chemicals and transmitting smells via electrical impulses to the brain. People have some 40 million olfactory receptors. Dogs have around 2 billion, which means they can smell between 1,000 and 100,000 times better than we do. Understanding the way dogs experience the world through smell can help save human lives. "Dognoseis," the process of identifying prostate cancer by training dogs to sniff out traces of the disease in urine samples, is one such area of research, but technology modeled on a dog's ability to smell is already helping us detect a variety of illnesses, from cancer to diabetes to schizophrenia.

In a broad sense, the question of what makes a dog a dog, or a tern a tern, or a human a human, is vexing. Vertebrates, mammals in particular, share many overlapping characteristics. Science is deft at classifying them. And observing the way other species behave—how they interact, communicate, adapt, and survive—has clear practical human applications. It's good and valuable in its own right.

But I'm not a scientist, and when I gaze into the deep of my dog's eyes or watch, perplexed and pained, the concentrated pacing of the leopard in the zoo, the central question, the most *human* and far-reaching question of all for me, remains: *Who are you?*

Many people (scientists among them) believe that animals are—if not "just like us" as anthropomorphism would have us believe—sentient to some degree. The trouble is, these same people argue, I can't prove it. Those who try often face philosophical quicksand. (Before you can say whether animals are conscious, intelligent, or emotional you have to define consciousness, intelligence, and emotion . . . and you have to answer questions like "How do we know what we know in the first place?")

One thing I do know is that people of every stripe—be it scientific, sentimental, or somewhere in between—care about the question. If human curiosity alone drove (and could fund) animal research, the study of animals' inner lives might be as brisk as the study of their observable behaviors. But for now those inner worlds remain largely mysterious. Their silence is resolute.

Modern Menageries

Zoos have always fared best in heavily populated urban centers where people live removed from nature and rural agriculture. On the heels of the new London Zoo, zoos sprang up in Dublin, Berlin, Frankfurt, Antwerp, and Rotterdam, and by the mid-nineteenth century, zoological parks had opened all over the world.

Though traveling animal shows and menageries were common in America by 1813, it was only after the Civil War—a period of growth, as the nation shifted from agriculture to industrialization—that money and resources went to developing zoos. Most imitated the European example, with postage-stamp collections and outwardly ornate buildings that were, on the inside, stark and easy to clean. The earliest zoos in America were at Philadelphia, at Central Park in Manhattan, and at Lincoln Park in Chicago.

As early as 1665, King Louis XIV had built a palace with gardens and a menagerie at Versailles. For the first time in the Western world, flora and fauna had been displayed together, and as foreign visitors flocked home with reports of the unique zoological garden at Versailles, it was imitated elsewhere. But as a rule, Victorian zoos took a taxonomic approach, grouping reptiles with reptiles, big cats with big cats, birds with birds. This was a handy method of classification, but zoo visitors saw the animals bereft of their natural context.

The first "naturalistic" zoo without bars was opened in 1907 outside Hamburg, Germany, by Carl Hagenbeck. Boasting moats, hedges, artificial rocks, and mountains, and incorporating trees, meadows, and serpentine walkways, Hagenbeck's design mixed species and presented pleasing panoramas of flora and fauna. It gave the illusion that predators and prey, humans included, resided side by side. His zoo was larger than others, and for the first time animals were displayed not taxonomically but zoo-geographically—grouped by zone—which helped zoo-goers connect animal, habitat, and ecosystem. This approach was both popular and influential, though some people claimed it positioned animals too far from visitors. By the 1960s, most major zoos could boast at least one naturalistic enclosure.

With interactive "immersion" exhibits, environmental themes, and a commitment to species management, today's zoos have evolved into conservation and education centers, using technology in the fight to preserve what's left of the natural world.

When the Endangered Species Act was passed in 1973, many zoologists realized the time had come to champion captive breeding and conservation. Zoos could no longer plunder an ever-shrinking wild world to replenish their exhibits and now saw their animals as part of a world gene pool. Reproduction became a priority. Problems associated with inbreeding inspired species survival plans (SSPs), in which participating zoos work together to save individual endangered species by assuring stronger, healthier offspring through breeding loans.

Certain animals, like the cheetah, don't reproduce well in captivity. And sometimes the captive population of an animal, as with the Siberian tiger, is greater than the wild one. Increasingly, we talk of zoos as "arks," and while captive breeding alone can't save the world's biodiversity, there have been genuine success stories: both the Arabian oryx and the black-footed ferret—once nearly extinct—were carefully bred in zoos and then, when the time was right, reintroduced into the wild.

Today sperm, eggs, embryos, and tissue from the world's most endangered species are stored in cryogenics freezers to safeguard genetic diversity. DNA fingerprinting, embryo transfers, egg

harvesting, artificial insemination, and captive release programs put zoos on the front lines in the battle to save endangered species, but the best zoos also ask what we're saving them for.

The "wild" is itself endangered, of course, shrinking the world over. It's up to zoos not only to safeguard species but to impress upon the public that, once saved, these creatures must be reintroduced *somewhere*. Conservation and education, then, are zoo imperatives.

Ideally a zoo visit is a mentorship—emotional, intellectual, spiritual—a way to interact with nature on a concentrated scale. It's the wide, wild world in miniature, and its human architects are conscientious stewards. The zoo experience should be, first and foremost, meaningful. There's too much at stake for it not to be.

But zoos are a paradox. Even as children, many of us feel there—together with our interest and curiosity—a muffled unease. People do have meaningful encounters in zoos, or they wouldn't flock to them in record numbers. I've had my share, usually late in the day when the crowds have thinned or gone, when the heat of the sun has waned, when the evening's meal is imminent and the animals know it, when I'm willing to sit alone—blank and patient and outside myself—and sit some more. But more often my experience has been representative.

If the animals are visible at all—not off exhibit or obscured by the very greenery installed to protect their privacy (and who would begrudge them?)—we watch through wire or glass, aching for a connection that rarely comes. Some children (adults, too) rap on the window or otherwise urge the animals on with funny faces and undignified attempts at cross-species communication. *Do something,* we think, and they do precisely what they will or won't. Natural antics—monkeys grooming or swinging in play—delight us, but familiar zoo behaviors like pacing, swaying, regurgitating food, or flinging feces evoke a vague embarrassment, as of some unwelcome intimacy. We may half-heartedly read the sign stationed to inform us of the captive's natural habitat and behaviors, but by now its unnatural fate may well have disheartened us. We seek solace in interaction, buttons to push and levers to pull, or we fix on some other distraction: tired toddlers wailing for ice cream, the heat, a blaring boombox.

In the end, novelty wins out over a tangle of emotions we can't name; that, or the tug to move on to the next exhibit, to the gift shop, to the snack bar, before our legs give out. In this way we carry on . . . consumers at odds with our own motives.

Perhaps we're uneasy because the animals withhold from us the one thing we would have: their consent. It would ease my spirit (prepare for some shameless anthropomorphism here), to be sure, if the wolf suddenly ceased its pacing, looked up, met my eye, and said, "Welcome, friend, and thanks for being here today. You see me, and it has changed you. I now see the worth of my sacrifice." But he will not pause. He does not look. I am unforgiven.

These are my own feelings, not representative of anyone else's, I realize. But zoos do seem to leave many people uncomfortable, maybe because—despite our best intentions—it's a lopsided exchange. We consume a healthy sampling of the world's biodiversity in an afternoon, and we make it home for dinner. But what do humans give zoo animals in return? The benefits of captive breeding. Basic care and protection (survival is no picnic in the wild; animals certainly have it easier in captivity). But is survival enough, and why is it ours to give?

It's an old controversy, and a circular one. There are as many ways to justify captivity (the animals have nowhere else to go . . . they're safer and better nourished in zoos . . . they're educa-

tional ambassadors here on behalf of their kind) as there are arguments against it. I have, with difficulty, weighted the scale first one way and then the other, and in the end I'm no closer to knowing than I ever was. I fear someday we'll regret what could not be helped, but for now I continue to see the intrinsic worth of zoos.

Two important ways they're still evolving are by offering more and more appropriate space and by anticipating animals' psychological welfare (not exhibiting solitary animals in confined pairs, for instance, or prey animals alongside predators, which may cause stress).

At a zoo in Florida, chimps use twigs to fish honey and jelly out of an artificial termite mound in the same way they might gather live termites in the wild. At the Bronx Zoo, keepers surprised the cheetahs by spraying different odors on logs and tufts of grass. At least one female turned out to have a strong preference for Calvin Klein's Obsession, sniffing out the log in question, pawing and rolling alongside it, even warning off an approaching male to defend her claim. Many animals naturally exude musk, and musk, it so happens, is a common component of perfumes and colognes.

This sort of stimulation, known as "behavioral enrichment," is a formal and growing science. Active animals are healthier, and one focus of enrichment programs is creative feeding, since most animals spend a healthy share of their time foraging for food in the wild. To encourage natural foraging behavior in poison dart frogs, say, keepers might conceal crickets inside a coconut drilled with holes. The chirping prompts the frogs to investigate, with the "alpha" or dominant frog at the fore just as it would be in the wild. Other possibilities include providing fish in screw-cap jars for octopuses or frozen rats bound in paper, grass, and string for birds of prey. Raptors seize and rip apart their prey in the wild, so the packaging gives them a chance to practice this behavior.

Together with chimps and other animals, zoo elephants have been known to create art. Paintings by Ruby, an eight-thousand-pound Asian elephant and former resident at the Phoenix Zoo in Arizona, sold for up to $5,000 in the late 1980s. Observing that Ruby often drew in the dirt with a stick to make her days more stimulating, her keeper bought her a canvas and easel, a selection of brushes, and jars of nontoxic acrylic paints. Ruby took to it right away, using her sensitive, many-muscled trunk to point out her brush and color selections. Not all captive elephants can—or choose to—paint, but paintings done by elephants have raised funds for resident zoos, sold at big auction houses like Christies, and have been shown in museums and galleries around the world.

The word *orangutan* comes from an Indonesian word meaning "man of the forest," but unlike humans and other great apes, orangs are shy and solitary in the wild. They may look like idle clowns in captivity, but they're clever opportunists, famous for their skill as zoo escape artists. They learn quickly by imitation and can plan ahead. A Sumatran orangutan named Fu Manchu—with a little ingenuity and a piece of wire repeatedly stashed in his mouth until just the right moment—made multiple daring nighttime escapes from the Omaha Zoo with his family. The group was discovered several mornings running up in trees near the elephant barn, where they lingered until a keeper could cajole them back to their exhibit. Other orangutans have staged escapes by using bamboo stalks or trees torn from their enclosure as ladders, or by disabling "hot wire" encircling their exhibits by covering it with rubber play tires or piled straw.

For some critics, enrichment tactics like these are exploitive and unnatural; they demean wild animals and warp or anthropomorphize their image for the public. This must surely be true, but it's also true that by removing animals from the wild, humans have altered *nature* as animals know it. Can depriving them, in the bargain, of stimulation or engagement—however artificial a consolation—do more than suit our own ideas of dignity? The goal of behavioral enrichment is to keep life interesting, and some more inventive captives have exceeded expectations.

In May 2004, the Detroit Zoo announced that it would become the first major animal facility to give away its elephants, Winky and Wanda—the latest residents in an eighty-one-year tradition—on ethical grounds.

In captivity, elephants endure unnatural climates and develop physical problems like chronic arthritis and/or psychological ailments bred of boredom and stress. Five U.S. zoos, under public pressure following animal deaths or suspected maltreatment, have closed elephant exhibits in recent years, but Detroit's one-acre enclosure is spacious, about sixteen times larger than American Zoo and Aquarium Association standards demand. The decision to move Winky and Wanda to a refuge was measured, precedent setting, and entirely voluntary. What triggered it?

In a public statement, zoo officials confessed, "We don't

phant greeting ceremony, which varies in kind and intensity depending on the relationship and on how long the two parties have been separated. Family members who've been apart a short while might greet one another with an exchange of trunks, raised or flapping ears, and throat rumbling. If they've been apart a few days, the greeting is more intense and might last up to ten minutes. Individuals run together, rumbling, trumpeting, and screaming, raise their heads, clack or entwine tusks, flap their ears, and whirl and back into each other. All told, the ceremony generates enormous energy and excitement, says Moss, who believes it maintains and reinforces the bonds among family members.

Elephant graveyards are a myth, but Moss once observed elephants kicking up the earth around a dead female and collecting branches and palm fronds to drape on the carcass. Females who've lost young calves may look "lethargic for many days afterward, sometimes trailing along behind their family," and elephants clearly recognize the carcasses and skeletons of their own species. Indifferent to the remains of other animals, they unfailingly pause and react to the body of a fellow, growing quiet and tense. They approach cautiously and inspect the body with their trunks. They touch, lift, and turn bones, running their trunk tips along tusks and lower jaw, tracing the hollows of the skull. "I would guess," says Moss, "they are trying to recognize the individual." Elephants may move bones as well, carrying them some distance from one spot to another, often near an elephant pathway or water hole. Even bleached old elephant bones will rivet a group if they haven't encountered them before. Are they remembering the past? Contemplating the future? Are elephants conscious of death?

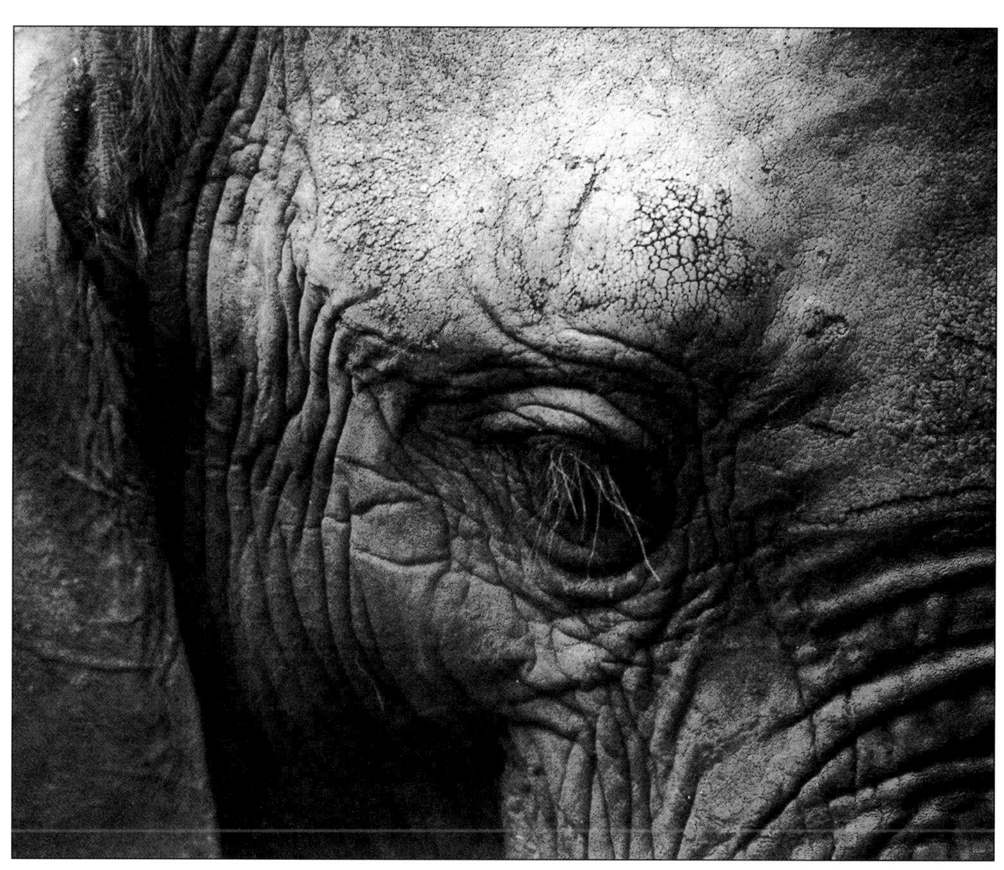

believe we can provide the space, environmental and social conditions that elephants need."

There's an old saying . . . that elephants never forget. What, exactly, do elephants remember? And should this matter to we who confine them? In the wild, Asian elephants like Winky and Wanda may roam thirty miles a day. They form unique, lifelong friendships with others in their herd. Like chimpanzees, they seem to be conscious of death and to mourn their dead.

Consciousness is difficult to define, much less study. Many researchers agree that it's more likely in "higher" social animals like elephants, chimps, and dolphins, which survive and thrive in groups by viewing themselves in relation to their peers. Complex social interaction calls for an awareness of self and others. But even bees create "mental maps," images they keep in mind that allow them to navigate around their environments by picturing themselves there. Are bees conscious?

In her book *Animals in Translation, Using the Mysteries of Autism to Decode Animal Behavior,* the animal behaviorist and advocate Temple Grandin, who also happens to be autistic, argues that animals, like autistics, live by what they see. They're visual thinkers, while most humans rely almost exclusively on language and logic, and as such suffer a sort of "inattentional blindness" to the wider world. The "hyperspecificity" of autism lets Grandin encounter the world more immediately and precisely, lets her think the way an animal thinks, in pictures. For this reason, she's called in by exasperated farmers and ranchers to spot the source of an animal's unease: often that turns out to be reflections in a puddle, or the yellow raincoat draped over a pasture fence. Grandin's insights have revolutionized the way slaughterhouses operate and led to more humane practices. She even makes the case that animals are autistic savants (in human terms, someone with an IQ very often in the mentally retarded range who can effortlessly do "genius" things no normal person can, like tell you what day of the week you were born based on your birth date). Animals are, she argues, far more able and intelligent than we credit because we don't read the world the way they do. We can't read the world the way they do.

What would they tell us if we could?

We're all separated from one another by our skins. We have a life outside, the observable life, and a life inside, which can be shared only if we're able and willing to express it; even then, the situation is complicated by the fact that we don't always know how we feel or can't articulate it. And what about those cases when what we say isn't exactly what we mean but comes filtered through rage, petulance, or pity? So we sit, inside our separate skins, and every now and then lean forward to gaze hard at another person and read his or her looks. We ask, *How's the weather in there?* And if they can

answer, if they so choose, we're privileged to share for a brief time what it means to be *other* than who we are.

Might it be that animals share—to varying degrees, inside their varied skins— these same shadowy contents from which love, terror, grief, compassion, and shame spring? Because they can't tell us, because we can't prove it either way, does that mean we should doubt what we see in our dog's eyes or feel in our gut when we watch the leopard pacing in her cage, when we catch the zoo elephant intent on a sound we can't hear, poised at a point of remembering . . . *what?*

Where We End and They Begin

One morning when Dionysus, the Greek god of wine, lay sleeping alone on a beach, he was kidnapped by pirates. The god did not wake till the ship was well out at sea, at which time he patiently tried to convince his captors that he was no earthly prince. The pirates only laughed at the regal stranger and sailed on, resolved to hold him for ransom.

Their laughter ceased when wine stained the sails with crimson blossoms. The air filled with the roar of leopards and the din of braying donkeys. The sea sprouted vines thick with grapes, which tangled the oars and engulfed the mast. Dionysus—now revealed in his full glory—watched sadly as one terrified sailor after another hurled himself into the waves.

But the young god took pity and would not let them drown. Instead, he changed them into dolphins, and that is why dolphins are the most human of all creatures in the sea.

I love this story—the idea of dolphins, with their expressive faces, being a lot of naughty, humbled pirates. I remember how disappointed I was to learn that the dolphin's smile is a glaring example of biased expectation (a form of anthropomorphism). Humans think of dolphins as glad and friendly because their mouths form a perpetual smile, but in fact dolphins lack the facial muscles to smile (or frown). Their "smile" is formed by the shape of their jaw.

Does this mean dolphins don't feel happiness? Can't feel it? No. But maybe expecting dolphins to be happy all the time (that is, denying them a full range of cetacean behavior, which includes aggression, stress, and frustration) is unrealistic or unfair on our part.

We would prefer to think dolphins are smiling at us because that means the moment shared was special; the connection was real. But what if an animal, wild or otherwise, doesn't return our regard. Does that diminish what *we* feel?

For me, art speaks to this need. The myths, folklore, and stories that fuel our popular understanding of animals spring from our deepest emotions about them. We may never really know them until they speak to us outright, or we become gifted enough as shape shifters to free them from the burden of our stories and expectations. But I doubt we could relinquish the way animals make us feel, even if we tried.

Where do wondrous tales of animals endowed with human or supernatural attributes square with the factual wonders of feather, blood, and bone, migration and echolocation? How do we separate the real animal—with its own unique biology and system of survival—from the animal of myth, legend, superstition, and symbol? And why bother?

With all the morphing that goes on in stories and the media, maybe, in our minds, true borders don't and can't exist. Maybe animals are us, and we're them, and that's that. We are animals, after all. Like whale and otter and bat, we're mammals, built of blood, bone, and fur. We nurse with milk and hone our instincts. We adapt, fight, and die. So there's little benefit—and much to lose—in positioning ourselves outside nature.

But on the other hand, a whale isn't an otter; a human isn't a bat. Can stubbornly casting them in human roles hurt other species? In the historical extreme, as we've seen, it's led us to burn animals at the stake, bring formal murder charges against pigs, and place parrots with the bad sense to parrot counterrevolutionary slogans on trial for treason. As recently as 1916, in a railroad town called Erwin, Tennessee, we sentenced and hung "Murderous Mary," a rogue circus elephant, before a crowd of 2,500 people. These are, of course, brash extremes, but they beg the question: How important is it to know where we end and they begin?

Animals are part of the emotional and spiritual fabric of our world. The relationship of spirit and science, owing to the extremity of the two poles, makes it hard for thoughtful animal lovers to form a healthy whole view, but it's worth a try, and I trust we'll never stop trying (however imperfectly) to know them, to tell and retell their story—which is as much our own story.

So I've restored the selkie to her skin, though I may need to borrow it back now and then. I love a story as much or more than anyone, require story as a means of understanding the world. But now again as I stand onshore among shrieking gulls, thoughtlessly plucking potato chips from a bag, I make a stab at shape shifting. I'm clumsy at best, but if I close my eyes, I can be a blue whale turning great slow arcs among the mountains under the sea, singing deep in the depths; an anemone blinking open and closed; an osprey soaring on thermals. I like to imagine, too, that on some far shore a selkie is wiggling out of her sealskin for just a taste—sweet and fleeting—of what it means to be human.

ACKNOWLEDGMENTS

I owe a great debt to the authors of the research books cited in the bibliography, on whose expertise I relied heavily. I'm also grateful to Gale and Karen Pryor, April Pulley Sayre, Meryl Brenner, Joni Soffron at Wolf Hollow in Ipswich, Massachusetts, and to the crew at the Cape Cod Photo Workshops. Special thanks to Lisa Goodfellow Bowe—always my first and best reader; to my husband, Courtney Wayshak, and our kids, Clyde and Michaela (faithful expedition-mate); to Roscoe, "Cupcake" Bradley, and all the other animals, not least the zoo captives, who've endured my company and my intruding lens so patiently. Thanks to my agent, Jill Grinberg, to the talented Michael Nelson, and to the entire team at Houghton . . . especially my bold and brilliant editor, Kate O'Sullivan. She is a rare species indeed.

SELECT BIBLIOGRAPHY

Adam's Task: Calling Animals by Name, Vicki Hearne.

And Then There Was One: The Mysteries of Extinction, Margery Facklam, illustrated by Pamela Johnson.

A Perfect Harmony: The Intertwining Lives of Animals and Humans Throughout History, Roger A. Caras.

Animal Behavior, edited by Tim Halliday.

Animals in Translation: Using the Mysteries of Autism to Decode Animal Behavior, Temple Grandin and Catherine Johnson.

Animal Talk: Science and the Voices of Nature, Eugene S. Morton and Jake Page.

The Beast in the Boudoir: Pet-Keeping in Nineteenth-Century Paris, Kathleen Kete.

Bees Dance and Whales Sing: The Mysteries of Animal Communication, Margery Facklam, illustrated by Pamela Johnson.

The Book of Beasts, T. H. White.

Capturing Nature: The Writing and Art of John James Audubon, Peter and Connie Roop.

The Chimpanzees I Love: Saving Their World and Ours, Jane Goodall.

The Covenant of the Wild: Why Animals Chose Domestication, Stephen Budiansky.

Darwin's Orchestra: An Almanac of Nature in History and the Arts, Michael Sims.

D'Aulaires' Book of Greek Myths, Ingri and Edgar Parin d'Aulaire.

Dogs That Know When Their Owners Are Coming Home: And Other Unexplained Powers of Animals, Rupert Sheldrake.

Elephant Memories: Thirteen Years in the Life of an Elephant Family, Cynthia Moss.

Elephant Slaves and Pampered Parrots: Exotic Animals in Eighteenth-Century Paris, Louise E. Robbins.

Every Creeping Thing: True Tales of Faintly Repulsive Wildlife, Richard Conniff.

The Feejee Mermaid: And Other Essays in Natural and Unnatural History, Jan Bondeson.

The Folklore of Birds, Laura C. Martin.

*Honey, Mud, Maggots, and Other Medical Marvels: The Science

Behind Folk Remedies and Old Wives' Tales, Robert and Michele Root-Bernstein.

If a Lion Could Talk: Animal Intelligence and the Evolution of Consciousness, Stephen Budiansky.

In the Company of Animals: A Study of Human-Animal Relationships, James Serpell.

Inside the Animal Mind: A Groundbreaking Exploration of Animal Intelligence, George Page.

Lads Before the Wind: Diary of a Dolphin Trainer, Karen Pryor.

Love, War, and Circuses: The Age-Old Relationship Between Elephants and Humans, Eric Scigliano.

The Mind Made Flesh: Essays from the Frontiers of Psychology and Evolution, Nicholas Humprey.

The Modern Ark: The Story of Zoos: Past, Present, and Future, Vicki Croke.

Monster of God: The Man-Eating Predator in the Jungles of History and the Mind, David Quammen.

The New Golden Bough, Sir James Frazer, revised and edited by Theodor H. Gaster.

New Worlds, New Animals: From Menagerie to Zoological Park in the Nineteenth Century, edited by R. J. Hoage and William A. Deiss.

Of Wolves and Men, Barry Hostun Lopez.

Once a Wolf: How Wildlife Biologists Fought to Bring Back the Gray Wolf, Stephen S. Swinburne.

The Oxford Companion to Animal Behavior, edited by David McFarland.

The Parrot's Lament and Other True Tales of Animal Intrigue, Intelligence, and Ingenuity, Eugene Linden.

Pliny Natural History, Volume 3, Books 8–11.

The Smile of a Dolphin: Remarkable Accounts of Animal Emotions, Marc Bekoff and Stephen Jay Gould.

The Star Thrower, Loren Eiseley.

The Tower Menagerie: The Amazing 600-Year History of the Royal Collection of Wild and Ferocious Beasts Kept at the Tower of London, Daniel Hahn.

What's Lost, What's Left: A Status Report on the Plants and Animals of the Lewis and Clark Expedition, Kim Todd.

Wildlife in America, Peter Matthiessen.

Wild Minds: What Animals Really Think, Marc. D. Hauser.

Zoo: A History of Zoological Gardens in the West, Eric Baratay and Elisabeth Hardouin-Fugier.

Zoo of the Gods: The World of Animals in Myth and Legend, Anthony S. Mercatante.

Zoo: The Evolution of Wildlife Conservation Centers, Linda Koebner.

www.pbs.org/wnet/nature/animalmind/ (PBS Nature: Inside the Animal Mind).

www.new.nationalgeographic.com/news (National Geographic News).

INDEX